Probation Practice

Alison Jones
Brynna Kroll
John Pitts
Andy Taylor

PITMAN
PUBLISHING

PITMAN PUBLISHING
128 Long Acre, London WC2E 9AN

A Division of Pearson Professional Limited

First published in Great Britain 1995

© Pearson Professional Limited 1995

British Library Cataloguing in Publication Data
A CIP catalogue record for this book can be obtained from the British Library.

ISBN 0 273 61634 X

10 9 8 7 6 5 4 3 2 1

Printed and bound in Great Britain

The Publishers' policy is to use paper manufactured from sustainable forests.

Probation Practice

Contents

About the authors

Alison Jones has worked in a variety of settings within the probation service. She is currently managing a Family Court Welfare team but retains an involvement with social work education and training as an external assessor for the Diploma in Social Work.

Brynna Kroll is Senior Lecturer in Probation Studies at Brunel University College and an external assessor for the Diploma in Social Work. She has worked as a probation officer, guardian ad litem and court welfare officer and is the author of *Chasing Rainbows: Children, Divorce and Loss* (1994).

John Pitts is Professor of Applied Social Science at Brunel University College. He has worked as a practitioner, researcher and consultant in juvenile justice and is the author of *The Politics of Juvenile Crime* (1988), *Working with Young Offenders* (1990) and co-editor of *Developing Services for Young People in Crisis* (1991).

Andy Taylor is a Probation Officer and practice teacher. In the course of 14 years' experience in four probation areas, he has worked in most areas of practice including numerous specialisms. Additionally, he works as a part-time lecturer and trainer and is currently involved in producing training videos for students.

Alison Jones, Brynna Kroll and John Pitts are joint authors of *The Probation Handbook* published by Longman in 1992.

1

Probation: politics, policy and practice in the 1990s

In *The Probation Handbook* (Jones et al. 1992), we introduced readers to the nuts and bolts of being a Probation Officer in Britain in the 1990s. We looked at the structure of the service, its responsibilities, the roles played by POs and the methods they used in their work. In this book we have focussed on those areas of practice which provoke the most questions and, in some cases, the most anxiety as well.

Since the late 1970s there have been a number of books which have concentrated on a particular method or technique of 'offence-focussed' work (Priestley et al. 1978, Priestley and McGuire 1985, Ross et al. 1989, Smith et al. 1994). We believe that although these methods and techniques have their uses, in the real world of probation practice, the single-minded pursuit of a single method is a luxury which busy probation officers can seldom afford. We have therefore produced a book which focusses on the people who come through the doors of probation offices, the problems and potential they bring with them and the challenges and dilemmas they pose to probation officers.

Because we have chosen to get as close to this reality as possible, this book sometimes finds itself at odds with the politics, and some of the policies and 'official' practices, of contemporary probation. This said, we are not simply reporting on this reality. We have a point of view; some ideas about how probation arrived at its present predicament and some strongly held beliefs about the way it should proceed.

So, while the bulk of this book is about practice, in this chapter we want to present a picture of the politics of contemporary probation and, in doing so, to make explicit the values, beliefs and political and theoretical perspectives which inform this book.

❑ The road to 1995

Prior to the mid-1970s there was an implicit assumption in criminal justice circles that criminologists and probation officers were involved in a partnership. The criminologists, for their part, undertook research into the origins of crime and criminality and, on the basis of their findings, probation officers devised remedies for it. Criminology supplied the science, practitioners provided the technology and together they solved the problem. And then in 1974 Martinson produce what was then regarded as compelling evidence that this partnership had been fruitless; that, in fact, nothing worked:

> It does not seem to matter what form of treatment in the correctional system is attempted, whether vocational training or academic education; whether counselling inmates individually, in groups or not at all; whether therapy is administered by social workers or psychiatrists; whether the institutional context of the treatment is custodial or benign; whether the sentences are short or long; whether the person is placed on probation or released on parole or whether the treatment takes place in the community or an institution. (Martinson 1974)

Twenty years on, this assertion is being challenged but it is was not challenged at the time and this is probably because Martinson's findings fitted so well with significant political changes occurring in Britain and the USA in mid-1970s.

At root, these changes concerned a growing unease, across the entire political spectrum, about the relationship between the citizen and the state and what appeared to be a growing intrusion of state agencies into the lives of individuals. In the field of criminal justice this critique came from four different directions.

The liberal justice lobby

Emerging first in the USA in the mid-1960s but gaining ground in Britain by the mid-1970s the liberal justice lobby attacked the social work presence in the court for its capacity to make unwarranted incursions into the lives and liberties of offenders. Characterising the *social enquiry report* as a 'character assassination' and pouring scorn upon professional social work's claims to any specialised knowledge or expertise, the argument was often long on rhetoric and short on evidence and analysis (cf. Morris A. et al. 1980). Social workers were to be barred from the courts and solicitors and magistrates, armed only with their law books and good common sense were to defend offenders against the rampant professional entrepreneurism of social work.

Left-wing criminology

The left-wing criminological critique identified social work as the velvet glove disguising 'the iron fist of capitalist oppression'. In this account social workers and probation officers were unwitting agents who served only to blunt the edge, or blur the reality, of class domination. In its softer version, the left-wing critique located social workers and probation officers as the 'zookeepers' of deviance who imposed pernicious deviant labels upon people who were merely engaged in relatively innocuous behaviour, perfectly acceptable in its own cultural milieu, but unfairly stigmatised by powerful agents of social control. Whether they were postponing the revolution by promoting false consciousness amongst their clients, or lurching clumsily through the social world saying bad things about OK people, the left-wing criminological critique located social workers and probation officers as part of the problem rather than part of the solution.

Conventional criminology

As we have noted, the mid-1970s witnessed the abandonment by conventional criminology of its central project, the investigation of the causes of crime and the development of techniques to 'cure' or eradicate it. In the light of all the available evidence the criminological establishment came reluctantly to the view that, like the search for the philosopher's stone, the quest for an effective method of rehabilitating criminals was probably a lost cause. This "decline of the rehabilitative ideal" (Preston 1980), signalled a profound change in the concerns of conventional criminology. In this period it moved from an attempt to discover the causes of crime to the far less ambitious project of devising more effective methods of processing and managing adjudicated criminals.

One of the by-products of this change was to highlight the ineffectiveness of probation as a means of stopping people committing crimes. Over the next decade, the practice of probation moved steadily away from attempts to rehabilitate individual offenders, to do 'more good', towards strategies which aimed to manage the system careers of whole categories of offenders in an attempt to do 'less harm'.

Right-wing criminology

Much British and American criminal justice policy in the 1950s and 1960s rested upon two implicit assumptions. Firstly, that people's position, or status, in the social and economic structure determined the ways they behaved towards one another, and secondly that industrial societies were destined to evolve, either through conflict or compromise, into more rational, more equal and hence less criminal and more harmonious entities.

In his influential critique of the criminal justice policies and strategies of the 1960s, James Q. Wilson (1975) offered a more pessimistic account of the way the world worked and what, if anything, could be changed. Wilson, a right-wing intellectual who became Ronald Reagan's adviser on crime and justice, along with other like-minded criminologists, became a shaping force in Anglo-American crime control in the 1980s.

Until the mid 1970s, the notion of a right-wing intelligentsia was generally regarded as something of a contradiction in terms. One of the defining features of the political right in the UK up to that point, had been its anti-intellectualism, gut-level reactions on law and order and other emotive social issues, and political pragmatism on less emotive ones.

Up to that point, *conservatives* were people who strove to keep things the same and *radicals* were people who wanted to change them. Conservatives simply acted to secure their interests; it was the radicals who had a vision of a 'better world'. From the mid-1970s in Britain and the USA however, we witnessed the emergence of a radical right-wing intelligentsia, with a vision of a better world and a commitment to fundamental social change. This highly influential group embarked on a political, economic and intellectual crusade which had an enormous impact on Anglo-American politics and policy.

The right wing criticised the architects of the 'welfarist' criminal justice policies of the 1950s and 1960s for their notion that by a process of 'social engineering' a better type of human being could be produced, Wilson writes:

> *Wicked people exist. Nothing avails except to set them apart from innocent people. And many people, neither wicked nor innocent, but watchful, dissembling, and calculating of their opportunities, ponder our reaction to wickedness as a cue to what they might profit-ably do. We have trifled with the wicked, made sport of the innocent, and encouraged the calculators. Justice suffers and so do we all. (p.209)*

Right-wing criminology maintains that despite increases in crime levels the numbers of people actually involved in serious crime remains small and that they are different from law abiding people. The solution then is to identify this hard core of serious offenders and take them out of circulation. As for the others, increasing the certainty of detection and reducing opportunities for gain through illicit activity will suffice.

These ideas have their origins in the work of the utilitarian philosophers Thomas Hobbes and John Locke whose theories of human existence suggest

4

that human beings are rational creatures who are motivated by the desire to maximise their pleasure or profit and to minimise their loss or pain. Thus, for the rational being, crime is a viable option to the extent that it helps maximise pleasure and profit. The role of the state is to provide a justice system which inflicts sufficient pain or loss upon wrongdoers to persuade them, and "those neither wicked nor innocent, but watchful, dissembling, and calculating of their opportunities ..." that their pleasure and profit will be maximised only if they desist from crime.

Together with the other, complementary, strands of thought, identified above, these ideas had a substantial impact upon policy and practice in the criminal justice system in the 1980s and 1990s.

❑ Early Thatcherism: the rule of law

On her election in 1979 Margaret Thatcher vowed to "restore the rule of law", although at that point her ideas about criminal justice policy clearly owed more to the blood-curdling rhetoric of the home counties hangers and floggers than the theories of the right-wing American criminologists.

At a conference on juvenile justice in 1979, just after the election, Patrick Mayhew, a minister of state at the Home Office, borrowing a phrase from the Duke of Edinburgh, bemoaned "the rising tide of anarchy and violence threatening to engulf our shores" (DHSS 1979). In the same year, James Anderton called for 'labour camps' for 'young thugs' and William Whitelaw, the Home Secretary, promised to provide them, and in doing so, give previously unprecedented numbers of 'hooligans' a 'short, sharp, shock'. In 1991, by contrast, Kenneth Baker, the Home Secretary, responded to an unprecedented increase in recorded crime by accusing its victims of not taking proper care of their property.

Clearly, in the 12 years which separate these utterances, both the message, and the language in which the message was couched, had changed substantially. Arguably, the rhetorical flourishes of early Thatcherism had three main functions. They aimed to placate the vocal right wing which had been swept into parliament by the Thatcher landslide; they served as a demonstration of toughness to an electorate which had been wooed with promises of safe streets and they were an attempt to divert attention from an economy which was going rapidly downhill. In retrospect, the blood-curdling rhetoric of the early Thatcher years appears less like the announcement of a new, pugnacious law and order era and more like the last gasp of the hangers and floggers.

5

❏ Mid-term Thatcherism: cost-effective justice

By the mid-1980s, however, the economy had pulled out of its nose dive and many more cabinet ministers were sympathetic to the arguments of right-wing criminology and impatient with what they saw as outdated eye-for-an-eye conservatism. It was they who attempted to fashion a rational, cost-effective justice system in which hard core criminals were taken out of circulation and the rest were 'managed'. In doing this they adopted the radical, 'scientific' managerial style pioneered in Westminster and Wandsworth. Describing their 'mission' in terms of 'targets', 'minimum standards' and 'performance indicators' they were anti-union, anti-professional and pro-privatisation. They set themselves against restrictive practices in the police, the law and the prison service and within a very short space of time these professional groups, which had previously regarded Conservative governments as their ally, were talking of betrayal. This was full-blown Thatcherism.

It is therefore particularly ironic that, having alienated and enraged most of the established professional groupings in the justice system, the government established, what was in effect, an alliance with a previously marginal group of radical juvenile justice professionals in the voluntary and statutory sectors through the DHSS Intermediate Treatment (I.T.) Initiative (1983) (Pitts J. (1988), Nellis M. (1989), Pratt J. (1990)).

Between 1981 and 1989 the numbers of juveniles imprisoned in England and Wales fell from 7,900 to 2,200. Although the period from 1979 to 1989 witnessed a 25 per cent decrease in the numbers of children and young people in the age range there was a reduction in juvenile imprisonment of approximately 68 per cent. The projects developed within the DHSS Intermediate Treatment Initiative were a key factor in this reduction. What commended the 'Initiative' to the government and persuaded it to develop a similar strategy for young adult offenders within the probation service was the apparent ability of workers in 'Initiative' projects to co-operate with, and influence the sentencing decisions of, magistrates. The development of similar skills by probation officers, was seen by the government to hold the key to the resolution of the penal crisis (Home Office 1990). As John Patten (1991), then a minister at the Home Office, observed:

> (I want) to promote a cultural change not just in the probation service, but among the sentencing classes ... The punishing classes and the helping classes are now talking to each other in a way they never did before. (The Guardian, p.4, 12 April 1991)

❑ The renaissance of common sense

The major 'achievement' of the IT Initiative was to get the 'punishing classes' and the 'helping classes' to 'talk to each other' in this way. It was an attempt to develop a 'common sense', between the agents and agencies which constituted local juvenile justice systems, about the problem of, and the most efficacious response to, juvenile offending. The creation of just such a 'common sense' between probation officers, magistrates, judges, the police and voluntary organisations was the objective of the 1991 Criminal Justice Act and many of the other recent developments in the probation service.

The key factor in the construction of this 'common sense' were the 'no nonsense' correctional techniques developed within Initiative projects, Bottoms A. et al. (1990) have demonstrated that the confidence of juvenile court magistrates in these techniques was the single most important factor determining whether they used alternatives to custody or not. That there was never any evidence that these techniques had a greater impact on offending than other forms of social intervention appears to have done nothing to shake this confidence (Van der Laan 1993).

This result was obviously heartening for a government attempting to manage a penal crisis fuelled, in no small part, by the readiness of the adult courts to imprison young adult offenders (NACRO 1990). They reasoned that if the probation service could be made to develop the same kind of relationships with the bench that the juvenile justice workers had, reductions in the incarceration of young adults would follow. The problem was that the relationship between the probation service and the adult bench was a well established one and, according to some magistrates, had turned somewhat sour. There was, it seemed, little confidence in the ability of the probation service to offer a serious alternative to imprisonment. As Mair (1989) observes:

> The Green Paper too notes that 'not every sentencer or member of the public has full confidence in the present orders which leave offenders in the community'. And the Chairman of the council of the Magistrates' Association has expressed 'sadness and worry' that 'many magistrates and members of the public have lost the unquestioning confidence and trust which they had formerly had in the probation service. (pp.6-7)

Beyond this, many people involved with the IT Initiative maintain that a significant element in its success was an acceptance on the part of sentencers that young offenders, by dint of age and immaturity, would simply 'grow out of crime' (Rutherford A. 1986). Whether, therefore, similar strategies could be used to divert older offenders from custody was an open question:

7

Unlike juveniles, young adult offenders suffer from unemployment and homelessness, they may be married, have children, and are more likely to be involved in drug use. Factors such as this mean that juvenile justice initiatives cannot be replicated unproblematically with respect to 17-20 year old offenders. (Mair 1989, p.8)

In an attempt to shore up the plausibility of the 1991 Criminal Justice Act the Home Office instituted a research and monitoring strategy (Mair 1989), introduced rigorous National Standards (1992) and produced weighty Approved Training Materials (1992), which included a, subsequently withdrawn, video in which a 'probation officer', who bore a remarkable resemblance to Virginia Bottomley, interviewed an 'offender' who was a 'dead ringer' for Sinead O'Connor. These moves aimed to proceduralise practice, identify key 'competences' and persuade the customers, the magistrates, that they were going to get what they had bargained for.

At this juncture, the 'nothing works' orthodoxy, which had held sway for almost two decades, appeared to pose a formidable barrier to the politically necessary rehabilitation of rehabilitation. But not for long. Criminology, always a pragmatic science, came to the rescue. Blagg and Smith (1989) write:

The outcome research of the 1970s was capable of being interpreted in other ways than 'Nothing Works' ... This has recently led some writers ... to argue that the pessimistic conclusion drawn from this research were not justified. (p.86)

This 're-interpretation' marked the biggest criminological U-turn since the admission that murders eyes were no closer together than other peoples. It raises questions about the relationship between politics, policy, theory and rehabilitative techniques and how disinterested the science of criminology actually is.

❏ Correctional technologies, political legitimacy and the rehabilitation of rehabilitation

'New' ways of working with offenders are not always a simple by-product of scientific progress or the proven efficacy of a particular method or technique. In the period since 1979, those methods and techniques which have gained currency in juvenile justice and probation have been a product of a complex, albeit largely implicit, 'negotiation' between politicians, policy-makers, theorists and, to a much lesser extent, practitioners. Indeed, we could say that these methods and techniques are a product of these negotiations. As Michel Foucault (1972) has observed:

... there is no power relation without correlative constitution of a field of knowledge, nor any knowledge that does not pre-suppose and constitute at the same time power relations. (L'Arc 49, pp.3-10)

Thus constituted, these scientific theories and techniques contribute a prestigious form of 'scientific' validation to what is essentially a pragmatic political endeavour.

Twenty years after 'welfarist' technologies of rehabilitation were declared dead we witnessed the renaissance of a new set of 'justice model' technologies which were congruent with the ideology of right wing criminology and fitted neatly into the new administrative arrangements. By abandoning those perspectives which address the personal, cultural, social, economic and racial factors which may increase the vulnerability of young people to involvement in crime or heightened surveillance by the police, the justice model provided a means whereby the political objective of a rational, manageable and cost-effective penal system might be realised. What the justice model lacked in explanatory power and rehabilitative impact, it made up for in political plausibility (Van der Laan 1994).

❑ The end of the boom

Until the beginning of the 1990s, aided and abetted by the justice model, the government seemed content to operate a rationalised criminal justice system in which practice was informed by ideological imperatives rather than evidence about what might work. This was a system in which cost-effective reductions in the imprisoned population were achieved by stealth. It was a system of justice which appeared to be utterly unresponsive, indeed unrelated, to the crime and disorder happening out in the world.

For roughly six years, from 1983 to 1989, periodic small-scale backbench revolts notwithstanding, the issue of crime was effectively kept on the back burner by the Conservative government. This is the more remarkable when we remember that the 1980s and early 1990s witnessed social disorder amongst young people on an unprecedented scale. It was the decade in which, with increasing frequency, working class young people from 'areas of disrepute' took to the streets of British towns and cities, with bricks, home-made fire bombs and, latterly, firearms, to do battle with one another and the police (Campbell 1993). It was also the decade which witnessed an unprecedented increase in the rate of recorded crime.

However, from 1988 the economy went into recession and as it deepened, crime in general, and the behaviour of young people in particular, was

9

dragged back onto the agendas of the major political parties. As the discourse on youth crime developed and tougher legislation was mooted, the courts anticipated future changes by reversing the downward trend in imprisonment of the 1980s and imposing more custodial sentences on juveniles. In 1991 there were riots in Cardiff, Oxford and Tyneside. Terms like 'bail bandits', 'ram raiders' and 'twockers' entered the language, displacing the 'muggers', 'hooligans' and 'lager louts' of yesteryear, and there was an 11 per cent increase in the numbers of young people sentenced to jail.

By 1992 the promised economic recovery still had not materialised and the government became even more vitriolic in its condemnation of young offenders. At the end of 1992 a 14 year old boy was shot dead in Manchester's Moss Side, the apparently innocent victim of the 'crack wars'. Also in Manchester, a 15 year old girl was abducted, imprisoned and eventually tortured to death by her 'friends'. In South London, a 12 year old boy was stabbed in his school playground. Alongside these events, the press was bemoaning the dramatic increase in live births out of wedlock in Britain which had risen from 11 per cent to 17 per cent in the 1980s. They reported record increases in the crime rate and record increases in youth unemployment and in February 1993 they reported the horrific death of two year old Jamie Bulger at the hands of two ten year old boys. On the same day, a *Daily Telegraph* survey indicated that for the first time ever, more Britons wanted to emigrate than stay in this country. Worse still, most of them weren't particularly concerned about where they would go, they just wanted to leave.

❑ Political reaction and instant expertise

The government was thrown off balance by the vehemence of the reaction to these events and the opposition had a field day. Tony Blair the Labour Party shadow Home Secretary demanded a regime of 'tough love', a phrase he had borrowed from Bill Clinton, in which containment and confrontation in 'secure units' would be tempered with responsiveness to the offender's needs. Ken Livingstone advocated longer prison sentences, and David Blunkett, shadow Health Secretary, called for *National Service*. John Major replied that we should 'understand less and condemn more' although he did not reveal what it was that he understood.

It suddenly appeared as if politicians across the entire political spectrum had felt for the last ten years that things, particularly juvenile things, were 'getting out of hand'. The dramatic re-moralisation of youth crime and youth justice was underway and this time the political left and centre were determined to wrest the political issue of 'law and order' from the grasp of the Tories if they possibly could.

The media had a field-day. A small army of professional and scientific 'experts' was wheeled in to chart the descent from a society characterised by civility and conformity to the contemporary moral quagmire. More than a smattering of these 'experts' were drawn from the radical right but the story which emerged was similar whether it came from the lips of a right-wing libertarian sociologist or a social democratic child psychiatrist.

Most of them identified the abdication of responsibility for moral leadership by adults, parents, teachers and public figures, as a key causal factor. Beyond this, they cited a lack of vigilance about the videos and television programmes our children watched and a failure to give them the 'quality time' that they so desperately needed in this increasingly violent and morally perplexing world. The problem was an indication of where the parents and the teachers had gone wrong. The behaviour of the young was a portent of what was happening to our society and the even bleaker future we had in store. They bemoaned the demise of a "golden age of parenting" (Pearson 1983) and they all called for a radical reversal of current 'permissive' policies. It was time to 'get a grip'.

❑ Getting a grip

In his book *Folk Devils and Moral Panics*, Stanley Cohen (1980) points out that moral panics emerge during periods of rapid social change in which social, economic and class relations are undergoing a realignment. Their function, he argues, is to attach the heightened concerns and anxieties generated by such change onto a concrete object which then becomes a 'folk devil'. In such a climate an act or an incident will serve as a catalyst to spark off the panic, after which discreet and unrelated phenomena are woven together in order to prove that things are, in fact, on the slide and that something must be done.

Kenneth Clarke, the Home Secretary, responded to he death of James Bulger by announcing the construction of a new type of Secure Training Centre which would house the 200 most serious and persistent young offenders in Britain aged between 12 and 15 whom, he claimed, were responsible for "60 per cent of the youth crime in the country".

As we have noted, the 1991 Criminal Justice Act was to have been the means whereby the lessons learned about limiting imprisonment in youth justice were to be generalised in all offenders. However, in an attempt to be seen to be 'doing something', Kenneth Clarke abandoned the unit fine system and the

11

regulations limiting the number of previous offences which could be taken into account by the bench. This had the effect of rendering 'irrelevant' previous offences 'relevant' once more and effectively sabotaged years of painstaking work by civil servants and justice system professionals who were attempting to inject some rationality into the sentencing process. Recent amendments to the forthcoming Criminal Justice and Public Order Act (1994), which will allow magistrates to commit young people in trouble aged 12 to 15 to already overcrowded local authority secure units instead of the planned Youth Treatment Centres, may well exacerbate the problem. A large influx of younger, 'sentenced', children into local authority secure provision may mean that the existing population, the majority of whom are aged 15 and 16, will be squeezed out, and hence up, into the penal system (Dennington 1991).

Taken together, these changes threaten to usher in a massive renaissance of imprisonment in general, and youth imprisonment in particular, in the middle and late 1990s. Estimates of the impact of these changes on the prison population suggest increases of between 5,000 and 10,000 per annum.

Yet, as Hagell and Newburn (1994) have observed, it is by no means evident that persistent offenders are also serious offenders and it is simply untrue that 200 persistent and serious young offenders are responsible for 50 per cent of all youth crime. However, the notion of a hard core of persistent and serious juvenile and adult offenders who are known to the authorities, and whose apprehension would usher in a low-crime future, is at the core of the policies which flow from the account of the world offered by right-wing criminology.

❑ The politics of policy in the mid-1990s

It appears that as we approach the millennium the government is using criminal justice policy as the means whereby anxieties about a faltering economy and its impact on social order may be assuaged. It aims to demonstrate that the natural moral universe is being restored by providing a shop window in which moral causes and effects are displayed. Of course, hardly anybody with the power to change anything really believes that the square-bashing, solitary confinement and slopping-out have any rehabilitative value. These tableaux of degradation are the symbolic foundation upon which the edifice of traditional conservative morality rests and the means whereby Conservative governments in trouble hope to restore their electoral fortunes.

❏ Trivialisation and the loss of professionalism

These developments have proceduralised the practice of probation and trivialised the contribution of the probation officer. Thus probation officers are prevented, or at least discouraged, from utilising their initiative and judgment to devise different, but relevant, solutions to the multiplicity of complex problems they encounter. This is not a plea for a return to an imaginary golden age of the probation service but a recognition that the move towards work with more serious and, in some cases more dangerous, offenders needs to be matched by an enhanced professionalism not a bland bureaucratisation (Bateman et al. 1991).

It is not that probation officers should not 'address' their client's 'offending behaviour', nor that they should shun the development of the social and cognitive skills necessary to a law-abiding life. It is rather that the factors which dispose people to violate the law are diverse, complex and often deep-rooted and, as such, do not lend themselves to a 'quick fix'. It is also the case that, the neo-utilitarian rhetoric notwithstanding, many of the people with whom the probation service works bring special problems of poverty, long-term unemployment and addictions, and sometimes long histories of abuse and abusive behaviour, which are not amenable, in any straightforward way, to the inculcation of social or cognitive skills.

The renaissance of the ideology of the rational, calculating and culpable offender has coincided with a steady increase in the numbers of people on probation officers' caseloads whose rationality is frequently or permanently impaired by their addiction to drugs or alcohol. Our argument is not that the methods and techniques which constitute the contemporary orthodoxy are intrinsically 'wrong', but that by presenting them as the answer to all the problems which probation officers and their clients encounter, they drastically over-simplify and trivialise the predicament of both.

By disseminating what is, in effect, a distillation of the good practice developed by probation officers, we hope to help to restore the balance. By describing the complexity of the situations with which probation officers deal, we hope also to convey the sensitivity and sophistication which good probation practice demands of practitioners. If the book does this, it will have succeeded.

REFERENCES

1. Blagg, H. and Smith, D. (1989) *Crime, Penal Policy and Social Work*, London: Longman

2. Bottoms, A. (et al.) (1990) *Intermediate Treatment and Juvenile Justice, Implications and Findings from a Survey of Intermediate Treatment Policy and Practice Evaluation Project, Final Report*, London: HMSO

3. Campbell, B. (1993) *Goliath: Britain's Dangerous Places*, London: Methuen

4. Cohen, S. (1980) *Folk Devils and Moral Panics*, London: MacGibbon & Key/Paladin

5. Curtis, S. (1989) *Juvenile Delinquency: Prevention Through Intermediate Treatment*, London: Batsford

6. Dennington, J. (1991) *The Mother of Invention: Negative Reform and Secure Accommodation*, in Dennington, J. and Pitts, J. (eds.) Developing Services for Young People in Crisis, London: Longman

7. DHSS (1979) *Getting on with Intermediate Treatment*, London: DHSS

8. Foucault, M. (1972) *The Intellectuals and Power*, originally in L'Arc 49 March, Paris

9. Hagell, A. and Newburn, T. (1994) *Persistent Young Offenders*, London: Policy Studies Institute

10. Harding, J. (ed.) (1987) *Probation and the Community*, London: Tavistock

11. Home Office (1990) *Crime, Justice and Protecting the Public*, London: HMSO

12. Jones, A., Kroll, B., Pitts, J., Smith, P. and Weiss, J. (1992) *The Probation Handbook*, London: Longman

13. Mair, G. (1989) *Intensive Probation in England and Wales: Origins and Outlook*, Paper presented to the British Criminology Conference, Bristol 17-20 July 1989, Unpublished

14. Martinson, R. (1974) 'What Works? – Questions and Answers About Prison Reform', *The Public Interest*, Spring, pp. 22-54

15. Morris, A., Giller, H., Szwed, E. and Geach, H. (1980) *Justice for Children*, London: Macmillan

16. NACRO (1990) *Young Adult Offenders*, London: NACRO Briefing

17. Nellis, M. (1989) 'Juvenile Justice and the Voluntary Sector', in Matthews, R. (ed.) *Privatising Criminal Justice*, London: Sage

18. Patten, J. (1991) 'Making the Punishment Fit the Frame', *The Guardian*, 20 Feb.

19. Pearson, G. (1983) *Hooligan: A History of Respectable Fears*, London: Macmillan

20. Pitts, J. (1988) *The Politics of Juvenile Crime*, London: Sage

21. Pitts, J. (1992) 'The End of an Era', *The Howard Journal*, Vol. 31, No. 2, pp. 133-149

22. Pratt. J. (1989) 'Corporatism, the Third Model of Juvenile Justice', *B. J. Crim*, Vol. 29, No. 3, Summer

23. Preston, R. (1980) 'Social Theology and Penal Theory and Practice: The Collapse of the Rehabilitative Ideal and the Search for an Alternative', in Bottoms, A. E. and Preston, R. H. (eds.) *The Coming Penal Crisis*, Edinburgh: Scottish Academic Press

24. Priestley, P., McGuire, J., Flegg, D., Hemsley, V. and Welham, D. (1978) *Social Skills and Personal Problem Solving*, London: Tavistock

25. Priestley, P. and McGuire, J. (1985) *Offending Behaviour: Skills and Stratagems for Going Straight*, London: Batsford

26. Ross, R. R., Fabiano, E. A. and Ewles, C. D. (1988) *Reasoning and Rehabilitation: a Handbook for Teaching Cognitive Skills*, Ottowa: The Cognitive Centre

27. Rutherford, A. (1986) *Growing Out of Crime*, Harmondsworth: Penguin

28. Van der Laan, P. (1993) *Dutch Penal Law and Policy: Notes on Criminological Research From the Research and Documentation Centre*, 02 1993, The Hague, Netherlands Ministry of Justice

27. Van der Laan, P. (1994) 'Alternative Sanctions for Juveniles in the Netherlands', in *Social Work in Europe*, Vol.I No 2, Aug. 1994

28. Wilson James, Q. (1975) *Thinking About Crime*, New York: Basic Books

2

Risk and dangerousness

Any probation officer who has the words of the National Standards printed on their hearts or tries to lift the contents of their in-trays, will know that the continuous assessment of risk and dangerousness is one of the cornerstones of good probation practice. As if the job wasn't complicated enough, constant references to risk and our responsibilities in relation to protecting the public can raise the anxiety levels sky high. We are reliably informed by our Probation Research Mole (PRM) that a direct correlation has been identified between the circulation of copies of the 1995 National Standards and increased sales of gin and chocolate.

The following chapters deal with the most challenging aspects of probation practice and the assessment of risk and dangerousness will be a recurring theme. It is easy to feel that as a probation officer you are carrying the responsibilities of the world upon your shoulders, that if anything goes wrong with anything, it is all your fault. Needless to say, although you may feel alone at times, this is in fact not the reality. You are after all part of a wider system; it is important that you do your bit well, but you are never solely responsible. There are many other players on the field and – let's be realistic about this – our clients, like ourselves, are complicated people living complicated lives, in a complicated world. To pretend that we can always build up a completely accurate picture and predict the future, is to deceive everybody concerned. This will remain the reality, until such time as the Home Secretary issues us all with crystal balls. In fact our PRM told us that these were on the way but, sadly, cash limiting has taken its toll and it has been decided that the Home Office's need is greater than ours ....

There are three sets of circumstances in which the probation officers might find themselves engaged in ongoing work with a dangerous offender:

1 With those on probation whose offence is *not* so serious that only a custodial sentence is appropriate. There may be additional conditions attached to the order which address the specific nature of the offending,

for instance to attend a project for sex offenders, a group for domestic violence, or counselling in respect of anger management.

2 With those whose offence was so serious that custody was warranted but whose risk of re-offending is sufficiently low to enable them to be released early on licence. Additional conditions may be attached to the parole licence similar to those attached to probation orders.

3 With those serving less than four years imprisonment who are released automatically on licence at the half-way stage, and those serving more than four years who are not considered suitable for parole but are released automatically on licence at the two-thirds stage.

Assessment is, of course, fundamental to all aspects of the probation officer's job and we are constantly weighing up issues of risk and dangerousness, to a greater or lesser extent. Indeed it is difficult to see how one could begin to help people to address their offending or to play a part in protecting the public were this not the case. The assessment of risk and dangerousness is central not only to working with offenders but also to the provision of information to others – notably the courts, the parole board and the Home Office.

Information for the courts

When preparing a pre-sentence report on any client the probation officer must, according to the 1995 National Standards, make an assessment of the risk of harm to the public and consider whether there are any community sentence options which might be effective in reducing the risk of serious harm (National Standards for the Supervision of Offenders in the Community 1992;1995).

Information for the parole board

All those serving prison sentences of four years or more are eligible for early release on licence once they reach the half-way mark of their sentences. Their case will be considered by the parole board (although the Secretary of State has the final say regarding those serving seven years and over) which must have particular regard to "the need to protect the public from serious harm from offenders" and "the desirability of preventing the commission by them of further offences and of securing their rehabilitation". (Criminal Justice Act 1991).

In considering a prisoner for early release the parole board has before it a dossier of numerous different forms and reports including a parole assessment report prepared by the supervising probation officer. In addition to providing details of the home, family and community the officer is required to make "an assessment of the risk of re-offending". (Prison Report Circular of 26/1992).

Information for the Home Office

In the case of both those on life licence and those conditionally discharged from hospital under the Mental Health Act 1983, the Home Office will require periodic reports from the probation officer who is responsible for supervision. Consideration of any potential or actual risk is of the highest priority.

❑ Assessment

Each of these instances will involve the probation officer in making a detailed assessment of risk and dangerousness, a complex task which is much easier said than done. Forensic psychiatrists and psychologists have struggled long and hard with this one. The jury is still out but most seem to agree with the statement that: "It is widely acknowledged that past behaviour is the best predictor of future behaviour" (Owens and Schoenfeldt 1979). Similarly most probation officers would probably consider themselves on pretty solid ground in concluding that a violent offender who had similar previous convictions would continue to prove a risk to the community unless something quite significant had altered. But what about those without previous convictions? It would clearly be very naive to assume that those convicted for the first time of a sex offence, a violent robbery or use of a weapon in a pub brawl, had not behaved similarly before. In order to make a full assessment it will be necessary for the probation officer not only to analyse in detail the offending behaviour but also to explore attitudes and fantasies and to gather information from others such as family and witnesses (usually via the documentation of the Crown Prosecution Service).

As 1995 National Standards remind us:

> Risk assessment is not a one-off activity; it should be undertaken systematically at regular intervals so that any changes in circumstances or specific new problems arising are noted...

Motivation is an important question to address – what was the incentive, if any, for the offender? A violent act may result from a variety of different motives and it is quite useful to ask ourselves a few questions:

- Was it an angry reaction to what was perceived as a threat or provocation?

19

- Was it racially motivated?
- Was it sexually motivated?
- Was it politically motivated?
- Was it related to a psychiatric condition or disturbance?
- Was it a means to an end, for instance robbery?
- Does there appear to be no motive whatsoever?

It is generally accepted that dangerous behaviour is the result of a complex interplay of factors including personality, early and developmental experiences, and structural/environmental factors. Certain factors will of course affect the likelihood of violent or dangerous behaviour and in assessing risk it is essential for the probation officer to consider those (sometimes referred to as facilitating and inhibiting factors) in detail.

Feldman (1977) suggested that those factors which have a bearing on whether an offence is committed include:

- Risk of detection – will I get away with it?
- Levels of punishment – what will happen to me if I don't?
- Levels of incentive or personal gain – this is a tricky one as it could include both conscious (for example money) and unconscious factors (for example power)
- Presence of a model – this relates to the individual's experience of others behaving successfully in this way.
- Emotional arousal – this relates to any strong feeling (fear, anger, jealousy, sexual desire) which overrides the usual mechanisms that control behaviour.
- Presence of disinhibitors such as drugs and alcohol.

In order for offending behaviour to continue, it is necessary for it to be reinforced. The sort of factors which act as reinforcers may be 'external' such as material advantage (maintaining one's Armani wardrobe by means of the odd bank raid) or social approval (being seen as the toughest, most daring member of your gang). By the same token, behaviour may be reinforced by internal factors such as increased self-esteem or reduction of anxiety through the release of tension.

This all sounds fine in theory but does it work in practice...?

Frank is aged 26 years and living with Sonia, his partner of two years who is expecting their first child in two months time. He is charged with ABH. During the course of an argument over whether or not Sonia should go to visit her sister (Frank preferring her to stay at home with him), Frank poked her in the arm with the scissors he was holding as she turned away from him, and the skin was broken superficially. Over the last two years he has been convicted of several violent offences. These have included common assault – hitting Sonia when she threatened to leave him, and criminal damage and assaulting a PC – he broke a window at his father's home when refused entry and subsequently punched the police officer who was called. He was also charged with threatening behaviour after he abused and threatened his mother-in-law who had told him that her daughter no longer wished to know him and has somebody else. Each of these offences was committed when Frank was drunk. He was out of trouble for three years previously when he abstained from alcohol. Frank is small in stature and was bullied at school. He describes his mother as cold and hostile and his father as overbearing and jealous.

Let's start by looking at Frank's motivation. It seems that his behaviour might be "an angry reaction to ... a threat or provocation". His violence tends to be associated with intimate relationships. In each of the instances there is a theme of rejection – his partner threatening to leave him or going out with her sister, his father refusing to let him in. It is possible that this apparent need for a close relationship and fear of rejection provoking a violent response is linked to his distant relationship with his mother and the role model provided by his father. The threat of rejection probably makes him feel very anxious ; the violent reaction reduces the anxiety, while at the same making him feel less vulnerable and more in control. It appears from Frank's behaviour over the last couple of years that alcohol is a significant factor in his offending, so there is clearly a 'disinhibitor' present. Also, it seems that so long as his drinking and the dynamics of his close relationships remain unchanged, he will remain at risk of violent re-offending. The safety of their new baby will clearly be a cause for concern.

Sandy is aged 25 years and is serving a three month sentence for an offence of affray. She and her mother had both been drinking and a violent argument ensued. When the police arrived they found her smashing crockery and brandishing a ceremonial sword.

She has numerous previous convictions for burglary and attempted burglary including an aggravated burglary when she threatened somebody with a hammer and an attempted robbery of a shopkeeper with an imitation firearm. The latter was very much a bungled attempt when she was so intoxicated that she hardly knew what she was doing and she was placed on probation.

Sandy was first cautioned for an attempted robbery at the age of ten and from then onwards demonstrated considerable behavioural disturbance. She abused solvents in adolescence and was excluded from school. At 17 she was diagnosed as having a serious personality disorder.

Sandy lives at home with her mother and two younger sisters, all of whom are very frightened of her as, much of the time, she is irritable and aggressive. She is severely agoraphobic, abuses tranquillisers and drinks heavily – the burglaries have been to fund drugs and alcohol. She has taken overdoses previously and has cut herself. She has no GP, having been taken off the list of several locally because of her threatening and abusive behaviour.

Sandy's story brings together a complex range of interrelated factors, and presents a very daunting, but familiar, prospect to any worker. It is not unusual in the case of a client who has been diagnosed as having a personality disorder or psychopathic condition to find numerous previous psychiatric reports in the file which conclude that the person in question is untreatable. It is often only the local department of forensic psychiatry which seems prepared to provide assistance and support to probation officers having to deal with what are often very worrying clients (see Chapter 7).

Questions about Sandy's motivation and what reinforces her behaviour are not easy to answer. Her behavioural difficulties started before adolescence and may very well be connected to family dynamics – her mother abuses alcohol and it is not clear what has happened to her father; both alcohol and drugs are problematic and presumably act as disinhibitors to some of her violent offending, particularly given her agoraphobia. They may, however, be seen as motivators for other offending – she may commit burglaries in order to keep herself supplied with drugs and alcohol. Sandy clearly poses a considerable risk both to her immediate family and to the public at large. The chances are that if these risks are to be reduced then it will be necessary for change to occur on several different fronts.

Derek is 32 years old and has served 12 years of a life sentence for manslaughter. He became infatuated with a woman at work who was friendly and chatty towards him but no more than that. On discovering that she was to marry, he followed her as she left the office and stabbed her with a carving knife. Derek is an only child brought up by both parents and his background is unremarkable and happy. He has no previous offences but there were several points in his childhood and adolescence at which he came to the attention of Child Guidance and the School Psychological Service. At the age of 12, for example, he put his hands around the neck of a girl. This apparently started as a joke but went further. When he was 15 he tried to push his best friend under a train.

Detailed assessments undertaken during his sentence have revealed that a feature of each of these violent incidents was his inability to cope with the realisation that his relationship with the victim was not an exclusive one. He experienced the presence of a third party in the relationship as a betrayal that he was unable to tolerate.

In relation to those serving long sentences probation officers are often in the position of having to make an assessment of the risk of re-offending when the serious offence of which they were convicted was many years ago and they have been removed from the community ever since. Detailed analysis of the offence, and of the previous situation and behaviour prior to conviction, remains crucial but fails to take account of any changes which might have occurred since. There has been a recent study of long-term serious offenders in Wakefield Prison (Clark, Fisher and McDougal 1993) which is of some help here. The researchers found that on the basis of the prisoners' offending behaviour they were able to predict what their behaviour was likely to be in prison with a high degree of accuracy. For instance (and somewhat superficially) somebody whose offence involved an assault against those perceived to be belittling or humiliating him is likely to be 'on a short fuse' in certain circumstances inside. Likewise the drug dealer who used violence and intimidation to gain power and control on the outside is likely to behave similarly in order to turn things to his own advantage in prison. The implication of this assessment is of course that a decline in 'risk-related behaviour' in prison may be indicative of low risk following release.

The extent to which Derek remains dangerous after 12 years in prison will of course depend on what changes he has undergone as a result of any work undertaken with him during his sentence. There will inevitably have been situations he experienced in prison which would have tested his capacity to cope with close relationships which are not exclusive – for instance with teachers, probation officers, psychologists etc. – and information about how he has handled these will be crucial. Of course, however well he handled things in prison, he will have to cope with additional pressures on release, some of which cannot be predicted or prepared for and there is always the risk that, when in a vulnerable state, he may be more likely to revert to previous patterns of behaviour.

❑ Working with dangerous offenders

We imagine that by now you will have got the message that assessment is the cornerstone of effective practice and you are probably wondering where you go from here. Irrespective of the nature of the order or licence, the work of the probation officer will comprise two components: **intervention** with a view to bringing about change, and **supervision** with a view to protecting the community. The balance between the two will vary depending upon the risk to others, the motivation of the offender, and whether there is any other 'change-agent' (such as a psychologist or psychiatrist) involved. However in all cases it is essential that a plan of supervision is drawn up which should be based upon a detailed assessment of all the risk factors.

Supervision plan for Frank

Frank has been made subject to an 18 month probation order for an offence of ABH against his partner, Sonia. Their relationship of two years has been a turbulent one with occasional outbursts of violence when Frank has been drinking. Both are keen for it to continue but his partner is adamant that this will not be so unless there is a change in his behaviour, particularly as their first child is due shortly and they are well aware of the risks of her/him getting caught up in the domestic violence.

Frank recognises that, if he is to change his behaviour, it will be necessary radically to control his drinking (he has managed this previously for a three year period) but also to attempt to break the existing pattern of his intimate relationships – he tends to be unreasonably jealous and possessive, to interpret the slightest thing as rejection and then to lash out. Rejection tends to follow which becomes a self-fulfilling prophecy.

The following has been agreed:

1 Frank to attend weekly sessions with the alcohol counsellor.
2 PO and Frank to meet weekly to focus on exploration of the pattern of his close relationships and how he might behave differently within them.
3 PO to liaise with midwife and health visitor in respect of potential child protection concerns.
4 PO to make monthly home visits to discuss progress jointly with Sonia.

Supervision plan for Sandy

Sandy has just been released from a three month sentence and her probation order is continuing. She recognises that her offending is related to her abuse of tranquillisers and alcohol but feels that it is only through drinking and taking tablets that she is able to cope. Specifically she identifies her turbulent relationship with her mother and her agoraphobia as problems. In our discussions during her period of imprisonment, Sandy has clearly expressed a wish to get some help. She recognises that her family are justifiably frightened of her violence and she is scared that it may escalate. Sandy acknowledges that although she does not like it, it is appropriate that the police be called in the event of her losing control and posing a risk to others, be this at home, at the GP's surgery or at the probation office. Her behaviour would probably be less extreme were she living away from home but numerous attempts to find alternative accommodation have proved unsuccessful to date.

We have agreed that the priorities at this stage are:

1 To make renewed attempts to find appropriate alternative accommodation. Sandy agrees that a period of assessment will have to be undertaken before she is accepted.

2 To establish regular appointments with the local forensic psychologist

3 To monitor and try to contain Sandy's use of tranquillisers and alcohol, which will be necessary if 1 and 2 are to be achieved.

4 To meet weekly at the office. Sandy agrees that if she feels unable to leave the house she will notify PO at the earliest possible opportunity so that a home visit might be considered.

Supervision plan for Derek

Derek has recently been released on life licence, having been in prison for 12 years. During his sentence he has had both individual psychotherapy and spent a period at Grendon Underwood Psychiatric Prison where he participated fully in the group therapy programme. He has developed a considerable degree of insight into his behaviour related to the offence, and over the years has moved on in terms of his ability to withstand emotional pressure within close relationships.

Derek recognises, however, that this is likely to remain a risky area for him particularly when he is likely to be lonely and vulnerable now he is released. Although he has begun the process of acclimatisation to life outside prison, as a result of a period spent in a pre-release hostel, he is aware that living, as he is, with a friend's family will inevitably raise issues for him about being included in someone else's family but not really belonging. While in prison Derek has qualified as a computer programmer but has not as yet obtained employment.

A plan for the first three months of the licence has been agreed as follows:

1 There will be weekly office visits in addition to which the PO will visit the family with whom he is living.

2 Derek will continue to seek employment and will attend the Job Search Project but will also explore the possibilities of a place on a degree course.

3 Derek will attempt to save £5 per week towards driving lessons and the PO will make application to a charity for the remainder.

Derek is aware that any concerns on the part of either the host family or his parents will be passed on to the PO and may need to be discussed with the Home Office. By the same token if he forms a relationship with a potential partner, she will have to be informed of his offence and in due course it may be necessary for the PO to meet her.

As with all offenders it is very important that supervision plans are shared with dangerous offenders. This is not only to record what has been agreed about the objectives of the work and how they are to be achieved but also so that the client is left in no doubt what in the probation officer's opinion are the risk areas and what action might be taken if there is cause for concern, such as notifying the Home Office in the case of a lifer or mentally disordered offender who has been conditionally released (see Chapter 7).

❑ Practice issues

Working with dangerous people who pose a risk to both themselves and others gives rise to enormous anxiety. As we said at the beginning of this chapter, it is easy to feel as though you have been left to struggle alone and that you, and only you, stand between an individual and their next terrible act. Lying awake at night wondering whether you have done enough and whether it was enough of the right sort of thing – what would an inquest have to say on the subject? – is one occupational hazard with this client group. Another is waking at dawn, wondering what will await you in your in tray – have Sandy and her family made it through the night following the crisis to which you were alerted yesterday? To ask the unaskable, as Prins (1986) suggests – has she killed either herself or her mother?

Many dangerous offenders have done something which most people would only be familiar with via the tabloid press or the TV screen. Probation officers get to know them well and have to hear every shocking detail. This can leave workers feeling contaminated and that their lives have been invaded in the most unpleasant way. Some dangerous clients are very intimidating and probation officers have to live not only with the fear of what they might do to others, but also what their client's response might be if the probation officers have to take action against them.

You will not be surprised to hear that very regular focussed supervision is absolutely essential if you are both to survive personally and to practice effectively with such clients. Senior probation officers are not paid their vast salaries to sit around drinking camomile tea and reading *The Guardian*, you know.

You need ready access to advice and information; you cannot be expected to know it all. You need to feel that somebody is sharing the responsibility with you and that they have endorsed your plans and actions. You need a forum to explore your personal feelings and what working with a dangerous client is doing to you. In addition, you need the opportunity to stand back from the work you are doing in order to ensure that you are remaining objective and on track and are not missing anything.

❑ Multi-agency work

It is very hard to imagine a situation in which it would be appropriate to be working in isolation with a dangerous client, although unfortunately this does not mean that it doesn't happen. It is not all that unusual for a court having been informed by a range of other professionals that nothing can be done, to call, in desperation, upon the probation service for help.

Even in these circumstances it is possible to mobilise appropriate support and assistance. Health visitors, community psychiatric nurses, forensic psychiatrists, social workers, GPs may all have a part to play and some may be able to offer more in a particular case than you can. Even if it is not appropriate for them to become directly involved in the work they can provide a valuable source of advice and consultation.

It is of course essential that the roles of all those involved are clarified from the outset. It is important that there is a clearly established communication system to enable information to be shared and that there is a mechanism for reviewing progress and the part each is playing. Different agencies will inevitably employ different systems of administration and may even differ slightly in their value base so we do not wish to underestimate the skills involved in effective inter-agency work. For instance, whereas you as a probation officer must pay equal attention to the needs of the client and those of the community, it may be that a worker in a therapeutic community will ascribe different weightings to the issues involved.

It will be necessary for you to use all your skills of negotiation, advocacy, tact and diplomacy! You will need to know what it will be possible to compromise on and what it is you need to hold firm on and you will need to be sufficiently assertive to get this across. If the forensic psychologist asks that you deliver Sandy to his clinic each week, you may agree that it is very important that she is assisted to keep appointments but might not consider it an appropriate use of your time. If you really don't think that other agencies are behaving appropriately or pulling their weight, you should refer the matter to your line manager who can take it up at a higher level.

Our clear responsibilities as probation officers for protecting the public mean that we are frequently in the position of having to pass on information to others to this end. Often it is clear cut, for instance, in the case of someone who has committed an offence against a child that there is a statutory responsibility to notify the local authority where they are living. Sometimes, however, it is not so straight forward and the decision is a difficult one. Let us imagine that a client with a serious mental health problem applied for a job as a life guard. That would certainly be one for discussion in supervision.

❑ Final thoughts

It is probably stating the obvious (you'll get used to this – it won't be the last time) but workers cannot afford to exercise the same degree of discretion with dangerous clients as with those who pose less of a threat. Any worrying behaviour, any unexplained missed appointment, any report from a third party which causes concern, must be acted upon immediately.

It is not uncommon for clients to fear their own dangerousness. They need to know that it is safe to share some of their most horrendous thoughts and fantasies without being rejected by the worker. If they are to feel that their dangerousness is 'contained' to some extent, then it is essential that appointments are regular and are not cancelled or changed without notice. This will be particularly important in relation to periods of leave when it might be advisable to ask a colleague to step in during your absence.

These are, of course, central elements of good practice in general and many of the themes we have addressed in this chapter will recur throughout this book in relation to different client groups. However, we cannot ignore the fact that the consequences of poor practice in relation to dangerous clients may be particularly catastrophic. So, on that cheery note....

REFERENCES

1. Clark, D.A., Fisher, M. J. and McDougal, C. (1993) 'A New Methodology for Assessing the Level of Risk in Incarcerated Offenders', in *British Journal of Criminology*, Summer 1993

2. Feldman, M. P. (1977) 'Criminal Behaviour: A Psychological Analysis'

3. Home Office (1995) *National Standards for the Supervision of Offenders in the Community*, HMSO

4. Owens, W. A. and Shoenfelt, L. T. (1979) 'Towards a Classification of Persons', *Journal of Applied Psychology*

5. Prins, H. (1986) *Dangerous Behaviour: The Law & Mental Disorder*, Tavistock

3

When in doubt, run – dealing with violence and aggression

- You are running an offending behaviour group. You noticed, when the group began, that one member – Felicity – was consistently silent, but waves of hostility seemed to emanate from her, and now, in week three, she seems to be a brooding, undermining presence. Other members seem to be intimidated by her, and this is seriously affecting the dynamics of the group. You know that Felicity has a very troubled history - she has been in care, and during her stay in residential institutions she damaged property and attacked both staff and residents. She is clearly in a very tense and volatile state…

- You are a woman probation officer and you are visiting Derek, (who we met in the last chapter), prior to his release on life licence. He has confided in you a great deal, particularly in relation to his infatuation with his victim, his feelings about relationships in general and his loneliness. During the interview Derek tells you that you are the only person he can talk to and how important your visits are to him. He tries to find out about your personal life, and when you side step this, he takes your hand and says, "I don't seem to be able to stop thinking about you".

- You are peacefully sitting in your office doing your records (!) when Frank arrives – yes, he was in the last chapter too – very angry because he has been refused money by the DSS. You have only met him three times so far, but you are well aware of his history of violence, particularly when he has been drinking. He storms into your office, swearing and waving his arms about, threatening to "do the DSS woman over" for not listening to him, and demanding that you do something about the fact that he has no money. He smells strongly of alcohol.

- You are interviewing Simon who has recently been remanded in custody for a PSR, having been charged with three offences of indecent assault. He

3905

has been very co-operative and has talked to you at length about the benefits of a previous period of psychotherapy which provided him with tremendous insight into his behaviour and motivation. Much of what he says is punctuated by buzz words and psycho babble and is delivered in a rather superior tone accompanied by a very fixed and intense gaze. In a confident and slightly amused manner he asks about your feelings about what he has done. He goes on to enquire about whether you have a particular interest in violent crimes – as a black woman, maybe listening to your white, male clients talking about violence is a turn on. You feel very uncomfortable – this man, with his smooth, smarmy manner, gives you the creeps.

These four situations – or something very like them – are probably all too familiar to probation staff everywhere. Encounters with different forms of aggression or threat are dealt with all the time, often to the extent that they are seen as such every day that they are not worthy of comment. Recent research indicates that probation officers have a one in four chance of experiencing an abusive or violent incident. Probation service assistants, hostel staff and family court welfare officers, as well as probation centre staff are also at risk (Littlechild 1993; Sheridan 1993). Workers are prey to different kinds of abuse; the importance of any definition of violence or aggression must therefore include the experience of the person at the receiving end. Weiner and Crosby (1986) underline this point particularly well:

> *If the worker experiences it as violent then for that person it will have been a violent incident. This also makes it possible to include incidents when sexism and or racism take place, as being violent for the receiver.*

This means that silent threat can have the same degree of impact as a physical attack. This is an essential point to remember, particularly when we begin to think about agency responses to incidents and the support available for staff. Some people will make us feel scared. There does not need to have been a violent incident before we bring this to someone's attention. We must feel able to share our fears and anxieties with colleagues and managers, safe in the knowledge that we will be listened to and what we have to say will be taken seriously.

In this chapter we want to look at the issues and dilemmas inherent in working with violent and aggressive people. What are the causes of this behaviour? How do we manage it personally as well as professionally? Are there any theories that help make sense of it all? What about organisational responsibilities – how should agencies be ensuring that workers are kept safe? How do we bear all this in mind, remain vigilant and take appropriate action without becoming scared of our own shadows, or needing three gins a night? What can we do to protect ourselves? What if the worst happens?

Working with violence and aggression has always been an issue for social workers, but it has tended not to get the attention it deserves. We have always had clients who lose their tempers, threaten, shout and sometimes attack. Sometimes we can anticipate events, sometimes not. Assessment skills become particularly important in this context, as we learned in the previous chapter. Equally important is getting to grips with the reality of the stresses and strains of clients' lives. There are often links between violent feelings and poverty, disadvantage, oppression, unmet needs and hopelessness. Many clients are close to the edge a great deal of the time. The desire to escape and avoid realities which are intolerable and feel impossible to bear often leads to alcohol and drug abuse, both of which can increase the likelihood of people reaching snapping point, sooner rather than later.

There is, of course, a new dimension added by the changes brought about by the Criminal Justice Act 1991, and the resultant changing clientele of the probation service. Higher risk offenders are being given community sentences; anyone serving more than 12 months in prison will come out on licence or parole. Probation officers will, as a result, be supervising people who have served long sentences for dangerous and terrible things, who may not want to report to a PO, but who have to. Workers will also encounter more people with serious mental health problems (see Chapter 7). This may be related to the impact of imprisonment, or simply the result of attempting to live in a difficult world where support is limited. All this taxes our assessment skills and, as we have already seen, requires that detailed attention is paid to evaluating the highly complex factors concerning risk and dangerousness.

What then do we need to think about and look for without, at the same time, making a host of assumptions? How do we realistically prepare for a range of eventualities without stereotyping our clients? Obviously not everyone who is mentally ill, for example, or uses drugs or alcohol is violent. Similarly, just because somebody has committed a violent offence in the past, or been treated violently themselves during childhood, this does not necessarily predispose them towards continuing violent behaviour. Present vulnerabilities and stresses are just as relevant to an individual's potential for violence, even if there is no history. Bearing these things in mind helps us to retain an awareness that any one could become aggressive or violent in certain circumstances. It is equally important to remember that it is not always possible to predict that an incident will occur. Don't blame yourself if you don't see it coming. You are after all only human!

❏ Myths about social workers and probation officers

It is dangerous to assume that, rather as a crucifix and garlic protects one from vampires, a Diploma in Social Work, or a degree in criminology (or any other ology for that matter) will protect you from attack. There is a myth abroad that we, as social workers and probation officers, should be able to do anything, anytime, with anybody, that we are all singing, all dancing, crease resistant, anti-static, offering hot and cold running love and care 25 hours a day… that we are never afraid and we can cope with anything. In fact, we are mortal and as liable to attack as anyone else – probably more so because we represent all kinds of difficult things that may spark off extremely strong feelings in our clients. In the last decade or so, the deaths of several social workers at the hands of their clients speak volumes about the dangers of this kind of work. They also convey some important messages about the limits of our own powers, as social workers, and the need at times to insist on the involvement of others, rather than be persuaded to go it alone. There is a limit to what we can do. The police and mental health professionals may also have an important part to play.

There is a risk for probation teams of adopting an institutional defence as a way of coping with the anxiety and fear engendered by their violent clients. This sometimes involves denial of the real dangers and the creation of a 'macho' culture – irrespective of gender – in which officers never admit to being afraid and almost go so far as to compete with one another in terms of how many unaccompanied visits are made late at night, how many dangerous clients they opt to work with, how often – and how late – they stay at the office after everyone else has gone home. This in turn may breed a culture of immortality, with officers sincerely believing that nothing awful could possibly happen to them. They are in effect cut off from the most effective ingredients of an accurate assessment of danger – good old, honest-to-goodness fear.

There is often tremendous reluctance to extricate yourself from a situation you know is dangerous. You may lose face, you may look like a scaredy cat in front of your clients, and your colleagues might not think you are up to the job. This type of culture makes it hard to tell anyone that you are scared. If you do pluck up the courage to do so, you may not be taken seriously, or you may run the risk of being labelled as neurotic or hysterical, inadequate or a weed. So much for the caring professions caring for their own. All this may make it much harder to take the sensible, non-omnipotent and professionally appropriate course. It is important to remember that allowing ourselves to become victims will not do our clients any favours.

Getting in touch with your fear is a good place to start. Fear was not invented for fun, it has a purpose. It tells you something important about what is happening to you and provides you with vital information about the other person. If you feel you are in danger, this is probably because you are. When in doubt, don't wait to double check that what you feel is real. Do something about it, and if you sense that your best efforts are not diffusing the situation sufficiently, don't hang about. When in doubt, run....

❏ What is violence and aggression all about?

There are all kinds of theories about why people become violent, and we will consider those in a moment. Reasons for aggressive behaviour can be complex and can include:

- issues to do with power differentials: power and powerlessness;
- gaining control when feeling helpless, hopeless, constrained by someone else's rules;
- testing out the boundaries;
- chaos, frustration, distress and fear;
- feelings of worthlessness;
- feelings of being uncared for.

Violent feelings are also evoked when people are treated badly or without respect. Brody (1993) highlights typical situations which fall into this category and are very familiar to us all – being kept waiting without explanation or excuse, being denied something to which we feel entitled, being treated unfairly in comparison with others, being treated rudely, being lied to or given inaccurate and ineffective information, being misunderstood and misled. All these are, of course, well worth bearing in mind when considering the experience of probation service clients.

Stereotypes abound about the potential for violence based on size, race, mental ability, mental health and gender. As workers, we have to be very mindful of not making assumptions on the basis of such characteristics. It is also vital to remember that our clients are likely to have been victim to such stereotyping previously and this will affect their expectations of what a probation officer thinks and feels about them. In such circumstances it would not be surprising for clients to be on the defensive and to present themselves in a way that could confirm the stereotype. For all of us anger is, in certain circumstances, a reasonable and appropriate response and is not indicative of violence and aggression. This remains so whether we are large or small, black or white, male or female, and irrespective of our sexuality, intellectual or physical ability or state of mental health.

Despite all the noble sounding policy statements that now adorn probation office walls, what we know about institutions suggests that they remain repositories of discrimination. It is obviously only actions and not policy statements which will have any real meaning for clients. These actions, of course, take place in the context of a relationship that is unequal in terms of power. This power differential between probation officer and client will in turn be influenced by differences and similarities – race, gender, age, sexuality, appearance, class and all the other things that distinguish us from one another. Both probation officers and clients are liable to make assumptions on the basis of these characteristics and if these are not made explicit and explored early on in the relationship there is the risk of serious misunderstanding fuelling what might be an already precariously balanced situation. For instance, if Frank's PO were also a young white man, it would be easy to for him to assume that his PO shares similar attitudes to women and their role in relation to men. If these assumptions have not been explored previously, then Frank may well feel misled, let down and even persecuted when his PO's response to his description of the way he treats Sonia is met with criticism rather than support and understanding. For some clients such an experience will precipitate violent feelings.

❏ Theories of violence and aggression

What about theories that might help us to understand where such violent feelings come from? Is it nature or nurture? Are we born with aggression and violence in us or are these feelings created? What part does environment play? Is violence learned behaviour? What about unconscious processes – where do they fit in? What about the chromosome argument?

Broadly, theories can be grouped into **nature** and **nurture**. The former includes biological and psychodynamic perspectives and the latter social learning and social psychological theories. They differ in their views of the development and maintenance of aggressive tendencies and how violent acts are triggered or provoked.

Biological theorists attribute aggression to physiological mechanisms which can override voluntary control. They put violence down to genetic make-up and personal pathology. They would see Frank as born with violent tendencies and having something seriously wrong with him There has been a lot of debate about chromosomal abnormalities as indicators of aggression (normal male = XY ; XYY has been linked to unusual aggressiveness). However findings have been inconclusive and Frank's genes (or pairs of genes) remain a mystery to us.

A classic representative of the biological school of thought is Lorenz (1966) who believed aggression to be instinctual – it preserves the species because it eliminates enemies, defends territory, and contributes to survival of the fittest (all rooted originally in the animal kingdom) … fight or flight is the central theme. If he accidentally knocked over Frank's drink in the pub he would therefore assume that Frank's violent reactions were survival mechanisms and nothing personal!

While Lorenz sees it as spontaneous, Morris (1978) sees violence as a genetically determined response to environmental factors. He contends that aggression can be controlled by innate appeasement gestures on the part of the would-be victim. Were he to meet Frank on a bad day, he would presumably bow, prostrate himself, or generally make himself smaller, possibly even sitting on the floor if threatened. Although this might baffle some of Morris's fellow drinkers, most social workers would recognise that such strategies as remaining seated, and using appropriate body language can be effective in the face of a risky situation.

Freud (1920;1955) from a psychodynamic perspective, believed that people had strong instinctual, albeit conflicting, drives – sexual and creative (libido) as well as destructive (thanatos/death). He saw aggression as the projection of the innate, self destructive urge or, "I'll do it to you to avoid doing it to myself". He argued that the inwardly directed death instinct was dangerous to the individual, but less dangerous if directed outwards.

Storr (1968) brings together some of these elements and looks at aggression in relation to various different stages of the individual's development. In addition he considers the impact of gender. He argues, for example, that aggression is often only aroused in the female of the species when their young are threatened – many a social worker is able recall the violent reaction of a mother when action is being taken which may lead to the removal of her children. More recently, theories of female aggression have centred on ideas related to the effects of being victims of violence, hormonal factors and the changing nature of women's role in society.

In contrast, social learning theorists and social psychologists see human behaviour as learned – otherwise, they ask, how is one to explain the fact that battered children often become battering parents, emotionally deprived people are likely to become aggressive adults, and those who have been loved and cared for are likely to love and care for others? They would argue that for those who have grown up with violence, it is likely to become a way of life by becoming a form of ordinary and accepted communication and response. Experiences of 'successful' aggression or aggressive models, for instance, parents who get their own way or gain power over others through their violence, make it more likely that aggression will be adopted by their children as a way of operating (Blackburn 1993). Thus, according to this 'nurture' model, Frank would be seen as the product of a family in which violence was acceptable and commonplace behaviour.

Such theorists also focus on the interface between the make-up of the individual and their social context. They argue that the pressures in our overcrowded, competitive western world, composed of those who have and those who have not, are probably more responsible for aggression than any innate biological drive (Hurrel Crook in Ashley ed. 1973). There is a tendency to feel that one must fight one's corner in order to have any value or identity as a human being. Aggression is seen as an attempt to restore threatened identity – we can probably all remember clients for whom this seems the only way forward when feeling challenged or threatened – for instance, by over reacting in a violent manner, when looked at oddly in a pub or feeling that a girl friend has been insulted. Someone whose sense of self is fragile, is more likely to perceive an innocent action or remark as in some way threatening. What is interesting, in this context, is that very often huge discrepancies are reported in the exchanges before a violent incident, with the aggressor often hearing something pejorative in words, tone or inference that the victim alleges was never there (Morrison 1993).

Theorists, working from a sociological perspective, focus upon class and subculture as important themes, arguing, for instance, that within some working class environments, it is through aggressive behaviour that young men are accorded status and validation. Campbell (1993) has linked crime and violent behaviour with recent changes in the structure of society. She argues that increased male unemployment has resulted in the occupation of, what has traditionally been considered as, 'men's space' by women as wage earners. Whereas previously, young men tended to grow out of offending and violent behaviour as they moved into employment, relationships and the creation of their own families (Rutherford 1986), increasing unemployment has meant that they now no longer have anywhere to go, in terms of this continuum. The result she describes is a chunk of society perpetually trapped in an adolescent subculture where identity is maintained through crime and machismo with a violent dimension.

❑ The management of violence and aggression

As the examples at the beginning of this chapter suggest, probation officers face a considerable variety of different types of threat and potential violence. It is of course important, where possible, to anticipate the risk and, once again, there is a range of possible questions we can usefully ask ourselves:

- Is there any history of violence?

- Has this person ever threatened violence?

- Is this person under an unusual degree of stress?

- Is this person experiencing frustration, perhaps unable to achieve something very important, however hard they try? Perhaps one step away from reaching a longed for goal?

- Does this person have unrealistic expectations of me or enormous unmet needs that I am expected to satisfy?

- Are drugs, alcohol or mental health significant here?

- Have I felt threatened by this person before?

- Is their uncontrolled behaviour escalating?

- Might there be a pay off from a violent scene? Is there an audience?

- Do I pose a threat to this person's liberty/children?

- Is this a particularly vulnerable period (just before a court hearing, just after release from custody, for instance)?

It is equally important to consider whether your client may have a particular reason to behave in a violent manner. Possible reasons could include relieving frustration, exerting pressure to get what is wanted – money, for example – or punishing either an unsympathetic system or an individual as representative of that system.

Sometimes, however, you can't anticipate risk, and this is the dilemma. There is no foolproof way of knowing whether or not you will be safe, no infallible guidelines or perfect checklists – this is one where you must constantly consider situations, assess risk and hope for the best. There are no easy solutions. Unpredictable people may include:

- bail hostel clients where histories may not be known;

- new PSR clients who arrive before their CPS bundles and 609s;

- clients' partners;

- people who appear in court for the first time and are unknown to the service.

In such instances it can be useful to remind yourself that this person is an unknown quantity and neither positive nor negative assumptions can be made about them. Once again, keep your antennae about you at all times – think about how they make you feel, and check the general 'temperature' of their behaviour and communication.

Let us return to our four scenarios and think about what factors might be present and how we might deal with the risks and diffuse the situation.

Scenario one: Felicity

This is clearly a risky situation. Felicity has a history of behaving violently and it may be that her violent behaviour when in care was something to do with the group setting. It could be that she is feeling insecure, vulnerable, intimidated and threatened by another member of the group, or feeling angry that she is not getting sufficient attention from the group leader. Clearly you cannot allow this situation to carry on, for everyone's sake – what are your options?

You need to convey a message to Felicity that you are aware that something is going on for her, that you are taking it seriously and she does not have to 'up the ante' in order for you to take notice – you've got the message. You could consider commenting in general terms about the atmosphere in the group, perhaps making some guesses about the reasons – "maybe people are feeling a bit anxious about what they are going to have to talk about today"; "it's always difficult to start talking when you haven't got the measure of one another"; " none of you had a choice about the other group members – maybe you don't like the look of someone here, or they have already rubbed you up the wrong way"; "maybe some of you just don't like groups, for whatever reason – a bad experience in the past, perhaps". Hopefully, one of these might ring a bell with Felicity and then you could go on to explore it a little further with her, showing interest and concern, actively listening, being empathic in the hope of diffusing the situation.

Scenario two: Derek

Most women probation officers have encountered a scenario like this. The impact is considerable and can leave one feeling violated, powerless and very vulnerable. The effects can be as intense as they are for any other kind of assault.

It seems clear that, on some level, Derek is emotionally deprived. It seems he is so desperate to have an exclusive relationship with somebody that no one could possibly meet his needs completely. His expectations of you, as his probation officer, are both enormous and totally unrealistic.

Derek needs to be given a firm message about the unacceptability of his behaviour and this must be given very clearly, with no room for misunderstanding. Having considerable sympathy with Derek's situation, it might be tempting to approach it gently and in a round about manner by saying something like, "Really this isn't appropriate, is it?" – instead of doing what is really necessary and making a direct and unambiguous request like, "Let go of my hand, please".

Once you have regained possession of your own extremities, it will be possible to start talking with Derek about the realities of your relationship and where the boundaries lie. Whereas it is neither possible nor appropriate to meet all his needs, there are, nevertheless, things you can offer in the context of the relationship you have built up.

Scenario three: Frank

This is another familiar situation, with some explosive ingredients – a client who is, to some extent, an unknown quantity, is verbally aggressive, threatening violence and he has been drinking. In addition, he has a history of violence and has come hot foot from a stressful encounter.

Any one other than Super PO will experience fear with all the physical symptoms that this brings with it – increased heart rate, dry mouth, shaking hands, shallow breathing. While all this is perfectly normal, it is important not to panic – breathing more deeply and an attempt to relax your muscles will not only make you feel a little calmer, but is also one of the ways of conveying 'non-aggression' to Frank. What we mentioned earlier about Morris's appeasement gestures is of particular relevance here. Remain seated and try to look and sound as relaxed as possible. Try not to raise your voice and keep your tone even. This isn't easy but breathing properly will help you keep the scream out of your voice. Ensure that although you make eye contact this does not become too intense, as Frank may well interpret this as confrontational.

Your successful handling of Felicity's group will have stood you in good stead here. Again, it will be important to demonstrate that you are listening to what Frank is telling you, that you understand the stress and frustration he is experiencing, and that you are concerned about his predicament and prepared to help. One would hope that Frank would begin to calm down, so that together you can begin to tackle the problem.

If this approach does not appear to be having the desired effect, you have several further options. A clear and direct request is a possibility, as with Derek. You may say, for instance, "Please sit down and stop shouting so we can sort this out". If this does not work you could say, "If you do not stop shouting I will have to ask you to leave and to come back when you have calmed down".

If all else fails, you have no alternative but to try to remove yourself from the situation and to get help.

However you decide to resolve this situation, it is essential that, at your next interview with Frank, the implications of his behaviour on this occasion are discussed. He needs to know that this approach to seeking your help is not acceptable and is unlikely to get him what he wants.

Scenario four: Simon

There may not be a risk that Simon will physically assault his probation officer, but his behaviour is nonetheless extremely aggressive and violent. Power is, of course, the crux of this matter and for whatever reason, he is intent upon being in control.

There are three arenas in which he has chosen to act this out – differences in race and gender and the knowledge he has acquired in relation to the probation officer's field of expertise. Simon's aim is to undermine his probation officer professionally, to intimidate her sexually and to humiliate her.

One's strongest urge would be to terminate the interview as soon as possible, get out into the fresh air, and to ask the senior to give the case to someone else, preferably a white man. However, to do nothing would simply be to collude and allow him to retain all the power.

It is very important to name the game and let him know that you recognise what he is trying to do and how he is trying to do it. If there is to be any change in this man's behaviour in the long term, then the themes of power and control will have to remain firmly on the agenda – a very wearing prospect for any worker, both on a professional and a personal level, since it will require this kind of regular and consistent confrontation for a long time to come.

❏ Issues for practice

There are three main issues to consider:

1 What should be done for you?

2 What you can do for yourself?

3 How to cope if the worst happens?

Agency safeguards – what should be done for you

You, as individuals, are your agency's most precious resource (yes, we know that they rarely mention this) and it is in their interests to keep you safe. Any agency which does not have health and safety policy and guidelines in place is not taking the welfare of their staff seriously and this needs to be challenged. By the same token, these should be accessible and available to everyone and not simply fished out of a bottom drawer when an incident occurs. It is essential that agencies maintain appropriate staffing levels, provide adequately for the training of staff in the area of violence and aggression, and monitor incidents. Appropriate support and counselling facilities should be provided and policies and procedures kept under review.

Now to the practicalities of a safe office environment. It is surprising how easy it is to wander into a probation office, unchallenged, or to be admitted through a marvellous electronic door, with only the most peremptory identification, or on the basis of an assumption. Our Probation Research Mole (PRM) reports the following exchange. Receptionist: "Have you come for the course?" PRM: "Yes". Consequence: a complete stranger gains access to the whole office.

Agency safeguards must include some basic preparation for all eventualities as well as basic advice about identification and checking mechanisms. Maintaining up to date records and having a system for speedily identifying those known to be a threat to staff will be important. Obviously, there will be people who call at the office who are unexpected and unknown. Finding safe and sensible ways of dealing with this situation is a prerequisite for safe agency practice.

The environment in which clients wait and are interviewed can help to create a calming or at least non-provocative atmosphere. People arriving without appointments may have to wait for what feels like a long time in reception areas and although bolted down seating is a wise precaution, anything that can be done to soften and brighten the environment would be very worthwhile. Two year old copies of *Woman's Own* do not always strike the right note! Security in offices and in interview rooms is important, but discreet measures such as hidden panic buttons and small windows in office doors are likely to be less provocative than for instance being interviewed through a glass screen or – as witnessed by our PRM – in a room without a door!

43

Ensuring that there are systems in place and adequate cover to deal with late reporting and potentially risky home visits is a management responsibility. However, the effectiveness of this in practice will depend not so much on what is written in well intentioned policy statements, as on a team culture which is underpinned by respect, co-operation and a professional attitude in which people are enabled to be honest about their levels of anxiety.

Staying safe – what you can do for yourself

In order to do your best work you need to feel as safe as possible, and there are certain precautions that you can take as a matter of course.

Within your own office it is not a good idea to have throwable objects, or anything sharp on display. If you have a panic button, it will not be much use if it is 12 feet (sadly, we remain metrically challenged…) away. Make sure that there is a reasonably clear passage between you and the door, so that you don't run the risk of being trapped behind your desk or falling over hat stand, waste paper basket and client en route.

If you are due to see someone who worries you, make sure you let a colleague know and arrange for them to be around and remain alert – all they need to do is pass by from time to time and listen out. Alternatively, get someone to ring you to check you are OK. There may be value in having a system of coded messages which is recognised by colleagues, although these need to be used with care, since the implausibility of, for instance, ringing reception to say you have left your car lights on on a bright sunny day may raise suspicions or antagonise further.

Now to consider home visits. Always fill in the movement board or office diary so that people know where you are going and what time you expect to return, and leave relevant phone numbers if available. If you are wary, and have to do a home visit, then take a colleague with you and visit in the daylight. Apologies, if this sounds like the most obvious statement you have ever heard. We make it simply because workers still take enormous risks.

How to cope if the worst happens

The adrenalin will keep you going for a while and then the full effects of being assaulted will overwhelm you. You will be exhausted on every level, be in a state of shock and will experience a range of different emotions. You may feel utterly hopeless, weepy, angry, disbelieving, sick, shaky, ashamed, guilty and responsible. You will pick the incident to pieces, blame yourself for not handling things differently or better and suspect that this is also the opinion of your colleagues. You may be edgy, nervous and afraid of the same thing happening again, for some while.

All this is normal. You will need plenty of time and space to talk about what has happened and to make sense of your feelings. It is important that a variety are sources of support are drawn upon. Friends, relatives, loved ones, colleagues and your line manager will all have a part to play. Despite all this, it may be that professional counselling is necessary and this is something that your agency should recognise and make available. In addition, questions of continuing work with the aggressor, criminal proceedings and claims for compensation will need to be considered.

❏ In conclusion

As we said at the beginning of this chapter, probation officers are only human and are not immune to the stresses and strains of everyday life. Just as you need to be aware of your clients' stress levels, it is also important to be aware of your own. We too have our more vulnerable than usual days – too much work, lack of sleep, personal pressures, threatening letters from the bank manager. We need to be aware of the ways in which we manage stress and how we might react if we are wound up to start with and someone turns that key a notch too far. By the same token, check your 'omnipotence' reading regularly to guard against the 'immortal, invincible, crease resistant' syndrome.

Listen to your own feelings – fear can be very useful – and give yourself permission to be scared. Finally, don't be Super PO… when in doubt run…

REFERENCES

1. Bandura, A. (1977) *Social Learning Theory*, Engelwood Cliffs, N.Y.: Prentice-Hall

2. Bandura, A. (1983) 'Psychological Mechanisms of Aggression', in Green, R. G. and Donnerstein, E. I. (eds.) *Aggression:Theoretical & Experimental Review*, Vol.1 New York: Academic Press

3. Blackburn, R. (1993) 'Aggression & Violent Crime', in *The Psychology of Criminal Conduct: Theory, Research & Practice*, John Wiley & Sons

4. Breakwell, G. (1989) *Facing Physical Violence*, Routledge

5. Brody, E. (1993) *Coping with Violent Behaviour: A Handbook for Social Work Staff*, Longman

6. Campbell, B. (1993) *Goliath: Britain's Dangerous Places*, London: Methuen

7. Freud, S. (1920/1955) 'Beyond The Pleasure Principle', in J. Strachey (ed.) *The Complete Psychological Works of Sigmund Freud*, Vol.18 London:Hogarth Press

8. Littlechild, B. (1993) *A Research Report into Aggression and Violence Experienced by Probation Staff in Hertfordshire*, Hertfordshire Probation Service/University of Hertfordshire.

9. Lorenz, C. (1966) *On Aggression*, London: Methuen

10. Morris, D. (1978) *Manwatching*, Penguin

11. Morrison, S. (1993) 'Both Sides of a Story: A Comparison of the Perspectives of Offenders and Victims Involved in a Violent Incident', in *Research Bulletin*, No.34, Summer

12. Norris, D. with Kenward, C. (1990) *Violence Against Social Workers*, Jessica Kingsley

13. Rutherford, A. (1986) *Growing Out of Crime: The New Era*, Waterside Press 2nd Edition 1992

14. Sheridan, M. (1993) 'Physical Violence to Staff', in *Probation Journal*, October 1993, pp. 143-6

15. Storr, A. (1968) *Human Aggression*, Penguin

16. Weiner, R. (1986) *Handling Violence and Aggression*, (Video and Training Pack) National Council for Voluntary Child Care Organisations

4

The highs and lows of working with drug problems

This chapter and the one that follows tackle some of the main practice issues that face probation officers dealing with offenders with substance misuse problems. While there are many commonalities – for example, theories of addiction and anxieties faced by the worker – there are also differences more specifically related to each area – the issue of disclosure in relation to illegal drug use, for instance. Whilst the division we have chosen is therefore somewhat artificial, we hope it helps to raise and clarify more of the difficulties under discussion. Clearly, readers interested in substance abuse will need to read both chapters, perhaps with a suitable break in order to indulge in their own favourite substance to keep them going….

The probation service has a strange relationship with drugs. There are some fundamental difficulties in relation to an agency that has a rehabilitative aim but is also part of the criminal justice system. Thus, many of the day to day dilemmas faced by practitioners reflect this dual and, sometimes, contradictory role in an area of work where most clients are in breach of the law by the action of their drug use alone.

Workers are beset by conflicts in terms of client disclosure and confidentiality and these will have a considerable impact on the whole process of intervention from assessment, through to engagement, to ending. Add to these child protection concerns, tensions regarding breach and inter-agency work, and you have quite a heady mixture.

Society's response to drug misuse, and the media's interpretation and reflection of this, impinges on the probation service's policies, and this has a direct effect on the front-line workers' response, not only in terms of trends (is there or isn't there a crack-cocaine 'explosion'?) and how these are responded to or resisted, but also how theoretical models develop and are suddenly pervasive.

Alongside this, workers have to deal with their own views, beliefs, fantasies, myths and stereotypes about drug dependency and they have to deal with these within a role where the issue of authority is central. Effective work in this area needs to take into account the workers' own views and responses and clients' anxieties and expectations of the probation officer's authority.

In addition to looking at the question of legitimacy, we will also look at the type of knowledge that it is useful to have in this area of work, whilst stressing that effective work is done by skilled probation officers not just people with specialist knowledge. Essentially, we will stress the value of working with clients to identify links between their drug misuse, their personal and social problems and their offending. Drug related offending is often a response to a potentially complex range of problems that the client experiences, rather than a separate category of behaviour.

❏ Drug misuse: 'a regular problem'?

The question of 'how significant?' was one that we were interested to answer, so we sent PRM out to investigate. When he came back he was so confused he had to lie in a darkened room to recover. On once more being able to face the world, this is what he told us.

Drug misuse, and the social problems and offending that often accompany this, are clearly a significant part of the probation officer's work. A recent Home Office survey (Nee and Sibbitt 1994) questioned all 55 probation services about their involvement with clients who abused drugs. The 31 probation services that replied estimated the number of offenders receiving treatment for drug problems on current caseloads. Most areas identified substantial numbers ranging from 1 per cent to 13 per cent of caseloads. (For example, 13 per cent in Middlesex 7 per cent in Yorkshire and 2,000 per year in Inner London.)

Other figures suggest that this may be an underestimate. A survey conducted by The National Association of Probation Officers (1994) reported that 50 per cent of crime may be explained by addiction to drugs and alcohol. The number of registered 'drug addicts' in 1993 increased by 13 per cent to 28,000, but this may be only a percentage of the actual numbers of users. The Home Office estimated that in the UK in 1990 there were between 35,000 and 90,000 heroin users alone. Jarvis and Parker (1989) concluded that perhaps 30 per cent of heroin misusers committed household burglaries, 24 per cent committed theft from the person, and that 41 per cent stole from shops (in 1987).

You can probably understand now why PRM was confused. The discrepancies in these figures make it hard to gain a true picture of illegal drug related offending. Part of the reason why gaining a clear picture is so difficult is because the link between drug use, drug misuse and offending is no simple matter. It is not simply a question of numbers as there is no straightforward correlation between drug misuse and crime. As Hough (1994) observes, whilst drug misuse and other forms of crime have causal roots in common, it is very difficult to say exactly how much crime is drug related because there are a 'variety of linkages'. He goes on to suggest that the popular stereotype of the casual user getting hooked and then being driven by dependence to property crime, represents only one example (perhaps a minor one) of the relationship between drug misuse and crime. Such a relationship may take other forms:

- Involvement in serious crime often pre-dates any problem use.
- Property crime can pay for heavy drug use and thence dependence.
- Property crime and drug dependence may increase in a vicious spiral.

Collinson (1994) introduces a note of caution with regard to the link between the two, in discussing research into young offenders: "drug use may often be one facet of delinquency, rather than its defining or motivating core".

While disputes rage about the number of drug related offences, practitioners in the field soon become aware that practice issues and dilemmas involving drug problems quickly present themselves in a variety of guises. The following cases illustrate some of these difficulties.

Pippa consistently makes 'emergency' phone calls to the probation office. This often occurs late in the day or before a public holiday. She is anxious that the probation officer visits her, but sounds so distraught that it is difficult to know the cause of the upset. She has been on probation before, mainly for shoplifting, usually to finance the purchase of drugs. She has used a variety of drugs over a long period of time. Her relationship with her partner is of particular concern, since despite consistent evidence of violence towards her, they remain together. If Pippa does not phone the office, her parents usually do, requesting immediate 'action' from her probation officer.

Trevor has just received a probation order for his fifth conviction of possessing heroin. The order was not recommended by the officer preparing the PSR, who had some doubts about what could be achieved in the face of his lengthy dependence on heroin. Whilst there had been aspects of the PSR interview that suggested that useful work could be undertaken and that there was some danger of Trevor receiving a custodial sentence, National Standards with regard to breach for missed appointments (albeit with some flexibility for those experiencing 'disrupted lifestyles'), led the officer to the conclusion that the client would simply fail to turn up on a regular basis, and would, therefore, be 'set up to fail', if sentenced to a probation order.

Adelaide left a drug rehabilitation hostel two months ago. She had stayed there for three weeks, not completing the planned four month programme but apparently making some 'good progress'. Whilst she was away, her partner looked after their four year old daughter. Adelaide was using cocaine prior to committing the offences of burglary and theft that resulted in her probation order with a condition of residence. After leaving the hostel, she returned to court in breach of the condition of residence.

These all too familiar scenarios begin to illustrate some of the practice dilemmas in this area of work:

- The anxiety of the worker that the client is not being honest about their actual level of drug use and that this may be masking more serious criminal activity.

- The difficulty of engaging with the client because of the clients likely perception that punitive consequences may result from revealing the real situation.

- The difficulty of making accurate assessments within the time constraints imposed by courts (particularly when defence lawyers may want to put a gloss on the court appearance as a 'turning point').

- The difficulty of trying to work effectively with people whose lives may lack routine.

- The stresses and conflicts imposed by this area of work and the attempt to keep at bay the influential view that drug misusers are always offenders, or that drug use is always related to chaos and lack of control.

- The tension between responsibility towards the client and towards other members of their family or the public, particularly where children may be 'at risk'.

❏ Have you worked with drug users before?

One of the main hurdles that can inhibit workers in this area is the worry that they lack expert knowledge. The fantasy can be that having detailed knowledge of the look price and cost on the street of, say, cocaine will somehow reduce the anxiety of working with clients misusing this drug. It is tempting to view such 'knowledge' as in some way offering security against the struggle of working with clients under difficult circumstances. From our experience, it is unlikely to do so significantly.

What type of knowledge is needed, if any? Do probation officers need to develop specialist techniques?

The newly qualified probation officer that took over Pippa's case soon found herself experiencing feelings of lack of confidence. This client and her family had been known to the probation office for over seven years and her previous officer, had developed a reputation as something of a 'specialist drug worker'. His knowledge of specific drugs, and local contacts seemed to imbue him with status in the eyes of some of his colleagues, and certainly in the eyes of Pippa's parents.

On taking over the case, the probation officer felt somewhat overwhelmed both by the complex history of Pippa's drug taking, as outlined in the weighty case file, and by the demands and expectations of Pippa's parents. They seemed to have a very clear idea of what Pippa's probation officer should be doing. At the same time she felt deficient in understanding the effects of the particular drugs that Pippa was using and this led to her feeling de-skilled during the early stages of their contact.

Although the case file had detailed Pippa's 'progress' from using amphetamines to taking heroin, the probation officer did not begin with a detailed discussion of Pippa's drug taking or history. Instead, she attempted first to gain a picture of Pippa as the complex individual that she was and this involved talking about her strengths, her skills, and her achievements, in addition to her position within her family.

In the second session, Pippa seemed more at ease and she and her probation officer began to look at some of Pippa's hopes and expectations, and how these had been undermined by feelings of anger and depression, which had resulted in her taking any substance that appeared readily available, via her circle of friends.

As the probation order developed Pippa began to identify more specific aims which, in her case, related to gaining a place at college, and developing a closer relationship with her brother. The probation officer discussed with her occasions in her life when she been successful in other ventures and looked at how this had been achieved. As a result Pippa became more confident about trusting her own resources, whilst her use of drugs, as an impediment to progress was often discussed, it never seemed to be the sole focus of discussion.

In this way, by using her generic counselling skills and more particular methods derived from her interest and experience of 'brief therapy' (George et al. 1990), the probation officer was able to help Pippa move away from her view of herself as the 'problem drug taker'.

The probation officer in this case found some of the ideas and techniques of brief therapy particularly valuable. This included looking at the time when Pippa had been in control of her drug use. The concept of 'problem free talking', enabled her to view her drug use in a different light, a problem over which she had more control than she imagined. It also helped to shift her view of herself from a passive victim, to someone who could take active control of her own life.

> The nature of most of the (social work) settings within which we operate means that there is a danger that we will connect with the 'problem' of the client rather than the 'person' of the client. The idea of problem free talk encourages the worker to connect with the person of the client and to begin to mark in the conversation, the skills, resources and strengths that the client inevitably brings. (George et al. op.cit.)

In working with Pippa, her probation officer was attempting to maintain balance. Clearly it was important to have some detailed knowledge and understanding of the effects of Pippa's drug taking and how this related to her offending. On the other hand, the methods by which she approached the work enabled her to concentrate on effectively working with Pippa as an individual, by avoiding the more stultifying and stigmatising effects of labelling. This had the effect of allowing Pippa to concentrate on her strengths and inner resources, not just her difficulties.

We need to remember the importance, therefore, of keeping the individual in view and when considering aspects of their drug use to see such behaviour as unique to that individual's circumstances and history. Again, this helps us to avoid making stereotypical assumptions:

> Substance dependency is not a peculiar problem of a tiny and different minority, it is a common life problem, experienced at different levels of severity, and in relation to different substances, by a significant proportion of the population. (Shepherd 1990)

It is important to choose appropriate interventions for individuals with differing experiences. Brief therapy is just one example of a useful type of intervention which seemed to suit Pippa. Others will require different approaches.

This does not obviate the need for information and knowledge in this area of work, as we outline below, but it does suggest that knowledge by itself will not make you a skilled drugs worker. Knowing the slang name for every drug and their possible effects may seem like the way forward but may indicate an attempt to over identify with certain aspects of the client, to fail to recognise the different roles you inhabit, and to collude with what they are doing. You will also look like a prize lemon if you get it wrong. The client's knowledge of drugs will probably be better than yours, and if you want to know a particular slang name you can always ask!

However, it **is** important for workers to keep abreast of certain areas of knowledge.

❏ Theories of dependence

This is the understanding of the processes by which individuals establish and overcome dependencies on abusive substances.

There is of course much debate about the causes of dependence, and these range from theories centred upon the 'individual', to those focussing mainly on 'social or environmental' factors.

Those theories focussing on 'individual' factors (i.e. those viewing the drug use as a result of a deficit emanating mainly from the individual, their family or history) include a range of different philosophical approaches:

1 **Psychological explanations** will tend to hypothesise that people tend to start to use drugs (and alcohol) in order to cope with underlying problems and that there are, therefore predisposing factors (e.g. early family conflict) which put various individuals in a greater risk category of misuse at certain times, for example, when they reach adolescence.

2 **Behavioural theories**, on the other hand, will stress the importance of why the behaviour itself (drug use) has developed and will focus on ways of thinking (cognitive). The idea is that people use drugs to gain positive outcomes due to lack of social or thinking skills. Behaviourists would seek to teach these skills in order to bring about these outcomes in legitimate ways.

3 **Social or environmental theories** will tend to view the deficiency in the environment itself, rather than the individual, and link motives for dependence to such factors as the need to escape from boredom, alienation, pain, frustration, meaninglessness, which is usually viewed as being engendered by direct social circumstances (e.g. poor housing, unemployment etc.).

4 **Other theories** identify the significance of society's confused position regarding drug use generally, for example, adolescents confusion over role models, the apparently arbitrary nature of drug criminalisation, and mixed messages in the media, advertising etc.. Such theorists might argue that better education may be one solution.

It is important to stress that such theories are unlikely to be pure, but are more likely to interconnect. Thus, for example, it may be argued that someone's use of heroin occurred as an indirect response to early childhood experiences (psycho-dynamic theory) which at a time of unemployment (social theory) led to them choosing a drug which during their adolescence they viewed as 'attracting kudos', and that the consequent learned cycle of behaviour, i.e. positive reinforcement of relief from anxiety, negative outcome of withdrawal, (behaviour theory) led to continued use.

But, whilst theories of dependence are unlikely to be discreet, it is important to keep in mind the particular weight given to each explanation, as these will often play a significant part in determining treatment responses. It also enables us to ask questions about why we are responding in particular ways and helps us examine whether such responses are appropriate and effective. Thus, for example, an over-predominance on social skills based groupwork responses may indicate a genuine desire to achieve consistency and effectiveness, or alternatively, a reluctance to address more fundamental structural issues (i.e. unemployment). On the other hand, an absence of practice models may indicate a reluctance to explore the emotional pain experienced by the client on an individual basis.

As we discussed in Chapter 1, different situations call for different responses, and an over concentration on a particular method or approach may give us some cause to ask the question 'why?'

❑ The goals of intervention: abstinence or control?

Generally, in the field of substance dependency, there is much debate about the most effective and achievable goals. Within this context, concepts of dependence based on a 'disease model' approach have come under a great deal of criticism. This is particularly the case where abstinence is viewed as the only determinant of real success. Some critics have argued that, as abstinence for many is unobtainable, approaches need to be more flexible and adapted to the reality of more achievable goals. Hence the proposals relating to a 'harm reduction approach'. However, it can be argued that such aims are not necessarily incompatible, and that abstinence may be viewed as one end of the spectrum.

A valuable body of material has developed which takes into account the different stages of dependence, linking this to decision making processes, and suggesting varying worker interventions at the different stages. Examples are outlined in the next chapter.

Trends in drug use

It is important to keep abreast of trends in relation to patterns of consumption, use and legislation as, again, these may help us establish more effective responses.

An historical perspective reminds us, however, that there is little new under the sun and that recent developments represent perhaps a continuance of underlying social problems being expressed through drug use, in different patterns or in different ways. As Berridge and Edwards (1987) observed:

> In the nineteenth century, public attention was focussed on the Fens and working class opium consumption in the industrial towns; in the 1980's, in Britain, the Wirral or Glasgow fulfilled a similar function. Public debate and discussion is still based on beliefs such as the inevitability of addiction, the impossibility of controlled use, and the moral decline associated with drug use, which had their origin in the anti-opium movement a century ago. The bogeyman 'drug dealer' has affinities with the racial stereotype of the Chinese and the opium dens. (Berridge and Edwards op. cit.)

But recent trends **are** significant because;

- We need to keep in touch with types of use and effects of drugs, to see how these link with current methods of education, prevention and intervention.

- They help to alert us to specific risks in relation to health (i.e. the link with people at greater risk of HIV, particularly in connection with prisoners).

- When there are new trends in drug use, these may often link to 'moral panics', which may result in new legislation or deterrent sentencing, often catapulting drug users up tariff, sometimes into custody at an early point of misuse. A recent example of this is the case of hallucinogenic amphetamines or 'dance drugs', where some recreational users have received custodial sentences for relatively small offences of possession.

Whilst we are clearly unable to discuss recent drug trends in any detail here, it is worth briefly drawing attention to some of the recent observations, debates and areas of research, which may be particularly relevant for practice:

- There continues to be a significant, long-term user population, particularly in relation to heroin and other opiates. As we have suggested, some heroin users continue to commit high levels of crime and at times of high unemployment, such habitual use may become a way of filling the void, which opportunities for work are failing to do. Thus, when drug intake is reduced or removed, consideration needs to be given to what may replace this (Parker 1994).

- Current research is drawing attention to new patterns of drug use amongst adolescents in particular. Thus, there is emerging evidence of complex poly-drug use and new types of 'drug careers' emerging from the extensive recreational drug use of young people (Parker *op. cit.*).

- There is a continued debate about the impact of crack-cocaine. Whilst the level of the problem and potential for far greater problems ahead is still unresolved (see for example Mott 1992), it is clear that crack-cocaine is highly addictive and, as a consequence, for some users leads to high levels of crime to support its use, and that there is an identified lack of available treatment responses. This is particularly true in respect of black people.

- There is evidence of an increasing problem in prisons with regard to high levels of drug misuse. There is current uncertainty about the possible impact of compulsory drug testing for drug users in prison.

Disclosure

This is a crucial issue, as this will often influence the nature and quality of the contact between client and the agency (and so client and worker). As Boother (1991) has stated: "If the probation service is to be effective in reducing offending amongst drug users, there needs to be a working environment to encourage a continuing process of disclosure."

An example of the problems encountered is illustrated in the case of **Trevor**. During the period when the report was being prepared, Trevor appeared relatively open about his drug use, which was used by his solicitor to support a recommendation for a community penalty. However, after the probation order was made, he became less sure about whether it was in his best interest to disclose a continuing problem with drugs, being unclear about the possible consequences of such a disclosure. Clearly, many of these problems are the result of conflicting agendas, the client perceiving that the worker will only help if they give up drugs altogether.

Harm reduction

Trevor's probation officer attempted to work within a 'harm reduction framework' as a way of reducing these problems. The 'harm reduction model' attempts to set 'achievable goals' which are more realistically geared to the client's drug use and history.

Harm reduction, as an approach, stresses that, for the foreseeable future, some people will continue to use drugs and it is therefore more realistic to try and minimise the harm which their misuse causes themselves and others. In this regard a 'hierarchy of goals' has been proposed, endorsed by the Advisory Council on the Misuse of Drugs (1991;1994) and expanded upon. These are:

1 becoming drug free,
2 switching from injecting to oral use,
3 avoiding sharing equipment.

These can be further broken down as follows, with number 1 as the ultimate goal, but with work beginning at the more achievable end:

1 facilitating cessation of drug use,
2 discouraging new recruitment into experimentation with drugs,
3 discouraging regular drug use among experimental drug users,
4 discouraging drug injecting among potential injectors,
5 promoting early retirement from injecting among current injectors,
6 encouraging regular injectors to switch to safer practices such as oral drug use,
7 ensuring that drug users have access to advice on safer sexual practices and safer injecting practices, as well as access to sterile injecting equipment and information about cleaning and using injecting equipment properly.

Harm reduction goals are also identified in the strategy for reducing the spread of HIV infection amongst injecting drug users, namely:

■ the stopping of users sharing equipment,
■ encouraging a move to oral drug use from intravenous,
■ a reduction in the quantity of drugs used.

The move away from abstinence as a goal towards a 'harm reduction model' has been a significant development in recent years (endorsed, as we have said, by The Advisory Council on the Misuse of Drugs, Home Office 1991) and such a philosophy has been adopted by probation services to greater and lesser extent. Although 'harm reduction' strategies often place central importance on reducing risks to health, they include looking at the wider aspects of harm and benefits which can take place in the individual's life as a result of drug use and are seen to have a direct application to the criminal justice system. Thus, the objectives in relation to health or wider issues are similar – reducing the harm caused by drug misuse to the community and the individual. The general aim is to move opinion away from a more blanket view of successful intervention being dependent on 'abstinence', to a more complicated (but potentially more optimistic?) view of the nature of drug misuse, and its relation to offending. It should be stressed that a broad harm reduction framework would not necessarily exclude abstinence as one goal for many, but it would argue against this as the defining measure of success.

Trevor's probation officer, was able to work through some of the initial difficulties, by acknowledging the pressures within his role and the position of the client. Working within a harm reduction philosophy, he was able to gain Trevor's trust and begin to discuss the pattern of his drug use, avoiding the assumption that this involved becoming drug free.

From this point it became easier to discuss the difficulty of changing long term habits, and to work with Trevor towards understanding what the benefits as well as the drawbacks of such misuse are. Most significantly, information about the problems associated with drug use, and unsafe sex, were also discussed and formed part of a preventive strategy in relation to high risk practices, that is:

- More openness from Trevor about times when he may have shared needles.
- Trevor taking more responsibility for using a condom on a regular basis.
- Discussion in relation to the views of both Trevor and his partner on having children and the implications of this.

Although changes may have initially been quite small, they began to represent permanent changes endorsed by the client.

However, whilst Trevor's probation officer felt that good headway was being made, problems arose following a supervision session with his senior probation officer.

Although some limited flexibility in relation to missed appointments was agreed (particularly as Trevor's response showed continual improvement), when discussing the detail of the case, it transpired that the SPO was concerned about Trevor's continued drug use, even though there was evidence that his situation had stabilised. The probation officer felt that, whilst lip service was being paid to the notion of harm reduction, the SPO was shying away from living with the difficult ambiguities that this produced. Thus the probation officer felt vulnerable in both recording and evaluating his work. By failing to support him in interpreting this harm reduction approach in specific, practical terms the officer felt that his SPO was impeding progress.

Effective communication in this area of work means not only being clear about the overall models within which agencies are operating (i.e. abstinence, harm reduction) and the treatment methods and policies which follow from these but most significantly, on a practice level, being clear about the way in which policy affects practice. The way in which the SPO's views conflicted with other harm reduction initiatives in his agency indirectly resulted in Trevor 'closing down' information. The confusion between revelation and response in the probation officer's supervision with his SPO was soon afterwards replicated in the dynamics between the probation officer and Trevor.

This dilemma was highlighted by the recent Home Office research into the probation service's response to drug misuse:

> The concept of harm reduction posed a considerable problem for the probation service, which worked on behalf of the courts to prevent offenders from re-offending and was uncomfortable with the idea of working with offenders knowing that they were continuing to use drugs. Individual probation officers occasionally worked with offenders this way, albeit somewhat furtively. However, it was clear that the conflict between the goal of harm reduction and current probation practice limited the ability of individual probation services to effectively address drug related offending. (Nee and Sibbert 1994)

The issues of disclosure and confidentiality are thorny ones in this area of work, and clarity with regard to these aspects is likely to have a significant effect on the progress and outcome of intervention. The more that goals, aims expectations and consequences are discussed and made explicit from the start of contact, the more productive such contact is likely to be.

This emphasises the need for specific probation areas to see that their policy statements on drugs are more specifically translatable to those working directly with drug using clients, particularly within the rapidly changing climate of policy and practice. In this context it is worth considering specific 'ground rules' in relation to issues of disclosure and confidentiality, that can then be negotiated more fully between probation officers and their managers and, consequently, between officers and their clients. These might include the following, many of which are from the very useful Northumbria probation service Guidelines:

- That the probation officer accepts that the client is using illicit drugs and is willing to work on the perceived problems that this produces, in confidence.

- However, any blatant evidence that the client is supplying drugs to others will lead to the police being notified.

- Similarly, any concrete evidence of offending to buy drugs (i.e. evidence which would lead to successful prosecution; stolen credit cards etc.) will also lead to police involvement.

- In some cases, a ground rule might be that the client receives a maintenance prescription for a heroin substitute so that the need to obtain supplies illicitly is at least reduced, if not removed.

Whilst it is acknowledged that such 'rules' need to be flexible for individual cases and circumstances, such detailed discussion between Trevor's probation officer and his manager may have led to more fruitful intervention at an earlier stage.

❏ Working with clients and referring them on

Probation services vary considerably in the extent to which they rely on the skills of external agencies as opposed to the skills of their own workers. (Nee and Sibbert 1994) and differ in the degree in which they have formal or informal arrangements with such agencies. Most of the probation services which use drug agencies generally use one of three main types:

- **Community drugs teams.** CDTs usually comprise specialist drug workers, community psychiatric nurses and a psychologist or psychiatrist.

- **NHS drug dependency units** tend to operate with a stronger medical emphasis and usually run both in and out patient services.

- **Drug agencies set up by the voluntary sector** are similar in composition to CDTs, but often put more emphasis on individual counselling and usually include a drop-in centre with on-site counselling.

In addition to this essentially community based provision, there are residential rehabilitation hostels, which vary considerably in the type, philosophy and length of the programme that they offer.

Following the changes to drug and alcohol treatment funding (Community Care Act 1990), clients and probation officers have had a far more limited choice when considering residential treatment – indeed, if any choice at all! It remains important nevertheless, for probation officers to have an understanding of the methods and philosophies of the residential provision under consideration, and to make time to discuss the implications of the kind of programmes with the client, enabling them, as far as possible, to make an informed choice about the decision to engage with a particular treatment at the right time.

When Adelaide's probation officer received a phone call from the court duty officer, he was dismayed to hear that she was due to appear that morning in the local Magistrate's Court covering the hostel where she had resided for the last three weeks. In fact, he was both surprised and anxious, as he had worked hard to provide a solution to what he had perceived to be complex and insoluble problems, some three months back.

At that time, Adelaide was in breach of a suspended sentence, with a history of shoplifting and two, more recent, non-domestic burglaries, involving small amounts of money. In interview she had said that the shock of this court appearance had made her reconsider her use of drugs. While sympathetic to her stated reasons for the escalation in drug use, the probation officer felt that he had to remind her of the possibility of custody and the seriousness of her continued offending.

In discussing the options, the probation officer was aware that Adelaide had had previous contact with the local community drug team. During a brief and hurried conversation with them, it seemed that they had been unimpressed by her attitude towards trying to control her drug use, and felt that whilst she "expressed a need for support, that she was more interested in gaining further drugs." The worker also stated that he felt that "Adelaide needed to escape from the pressures of the area, as she was becoming more involved in wheeling and dealing on the drug scene".

In addition to all this, Adelaide expressed concern and ambiguity about the state of her relationship with her partner, and was extremely worried about the consequences of a custodial sentence with regard to her four year old daughter.

Although the probation officer had seen Adelaide, her partner and daughter during a second interview, he remained confused and anxious about a number of issues:

- How serious was Adelaide's drug taking? If it was progressing to a point where she was selling drugs on a regular basis, what were the implications of this?

- In view of such ambiguous and apparently conflicting views of her drug use, how possible was it to assess the potential risks involved for the couple's four year old child?

- Was he in danger of underestimating the risks if he didn't look at the potential dangers? On the other hand, if he overreacted, was he not in equal danger of stereotyping Adelaide as an 'out of control drug user', who would place her needs above her childcare concerns?

- Was there value in trying to persuade Adelaide that she may benefit from residential treatment? In other words, could the reality of the seriousness of her position influence her decision to change? Alternatively, was she being persuaded into such an option because it seemed like a neater solution for the court, the probation officer, and the drugs agency? Was it just, in fact, deferring difficulties to a later date?

In the event, Adelaide received a probation order with a condition of residence at the hostel, some way from her home. Three weeks later she absconded. As a consequence, her probation officer looked back at their contact during the PSR process and reflected, with hindsight, on the following:

- To what extent did her reluctance to disclose her drug use relate to her fear of the possible consequences in relation to her child?

- Had he really gained a considered view of her progress and history with the drug agency in order to make a considered assessment? What contact had she had with other professionals?

- Would a joint meeting at an earlier stage, exploring the possibility for joint agency work, have helped clarify expectations on all sides? As a result of this, might he have been better placed to suggest a realistic 'sentencing package' to the court, without recourse to a residential condition? (This would have fitted more closely with his agency's stated policy of only proposing treatment conditions for serious offenders, or in exceptional circumstances.)

In the event, Adelaide was found to be in breach of the condition to reside for treatment. Subsequently, however, her probation officer was able to negotiate a joint plan of work with the local drug agency, and she was sentenced to a new probation order, without additional conditions.

To sum up, working in partnership with other agencies offers great potential. However, some of the following factors are worthy of consideration if such work is to be truly effective:

■ The need for clear and regular communication between all the agencies involved. This should ideally start from a contractual basis when a new agency becomes involved. Nee and Sibbert (*op. cit.*) suggest that, where there are child protection issues, offenders should be given clear information about the consequences of disclosing further drug misuse (in consultation with social services).

■ Agencies should be in a position to give feedback about clients to the joint working agency and drug agencies should be encouraged to gain consent from offenders, where such feedback is requested.

■ Probation officers need to have knowledge of the specialist agencies, other community resources, referral procedures and funding arrangements in their areas.

■ Probation officers need to have a working knowledge of treatment models and philosophies of different drug agencies and residential provision, so that as far as possible, problems and interventions are matched, and interventions are undertaken, taking into account cultural variables and personal belief systems (CCETSW 1992).

■ Workers need to be clear about their respective roles throughout the period of joint working.

■ Workers need to be aware of the importance of building on previous client experiences, identifying the positives achieved, particularly where the client may have perceived leaving a programme or period of treatment as a failure.

Before you resign, or reach for the valium yourself, we think it's only fair to point out that many of these debates, problems and conflicts are going to crop up again in relation to alcohol problems. So, grab a bar of chocolate (still legal, thank goodness) and read on....

REFERENCES

1. Advisory Council on the Misuse Of Drugs (1991 and 1994) *Drug Misusers and the Criminal Justice System; Pts 1 and 2*, Home Office

2. Berridge, V. and Edwards, G. (1987) *Opium and the People*, Yale University Press

3. Boother, M. (1991) 'Drug Misuse: Developing a Harm Reduction Strategy', in *Probation Journal*, June, pp. 75-81

4. C.C.E.T.S.W. (1992) *Substance Misuse; Guidance notes for the Diploma in Social Work*, C.C.E.T.S.W. publications

5. Collison, M. (1994) 'Drugs and delinquency: A Non Treatment Paradigm?', in *Probation Journal*, December, pp. 203-8

6. George, E., Iveson, C. and Ratner, H. (1990) *Problem to Solution: Brief Therapy with Individuals & Families*, BT Press

7. Gunn and Maden (1988) *British Medical Journal*, Vol 30; 302

8. Hough, M. (1994) *Problem Drug Use and Criminal Justice*, A discussion paper for the National Working Seminar on Drugs prevention within the Criminal Justice System. South Bank University 1994

9. Jarvis and Parker (1989) *British Journal of Criminology*, 29

10. Maddalena, N. (1994) *Drug Misusers Remanded in Custody* (ILPS Research Document June 1994)

11. Mott, J. (ed.) (1992) *Crack and Cocaine in England and Wales*, Research and Planning Unit Paper 70, Home Office

12. Nee, C. and Sibbert, R. (1993) *The Probation Response to Drug Misuse*, Research and Planning Unit Paper 78, Home Office

13. Parker, H. (1994) 'The New Drug Users', in *Probation Journal*, September, pp. 144-7

14. Shephard, A. (1990) *Substance Dependency: A Professional Guide*, Venture Press

The authors would like to gratefully acknowledge Fiona Bauermeister's contribution to the preparation of this chapter.

5

Message in a bottle – working with alcohol abuse

Alcohol is, of course, a legal drug (in Britain anyway), but how people use this and how they view others' use often depends on a range of factors, including their own history, personal, cultural and religious belief systems, and wider social influences and pressures. Working with alcohol is an area of practice which encompasses a variety of contradictory views and responses in reaction to an activity that is viewed both positively and negatively. Such conflicting responses affect how the probation officer and client negotiate alcohol related difficulties, in addition to influencing the way the relationship between alcohol use and offending is defined, assessed and judged. For example, drink drivers may, as a group, be particularly disapproved of by some, whereas some may view an entrenched drinker as suffering from a disorder over which they have temporarily lost control. These differing perceptions may affect the degree of concern that the behaviour may attract. There is continued debate in courts about whether drink mitigates or aggravates the culpability of offenders' actions.

Such ambiguity is particularly evident in society's often varying response to the type of drinking on view. Drinking is on the one hand seen as a social lubricant, often reflecting aspects of success and happiness and joie de vivre; whilst on the other hand 'problem drinkers' tend to be viewed as failures, who may be drinking in order to blot out their difficulties. It is interesting to ponder where the dividing line between these two images is meant to be. Alcohol can be seen to represent, in this sense, society's ambivalent attitude towards mood altering or addictive substances. Many probation officers will have reflected on this when, struggling to find suitable video material (with the inevitable poor sound quality!) for the next alcohol education group, they happen to catch the latest mega-buck production of a Bacardi ad at the cinema.

Alcohol related problems and crime have many facets and will appear to the probation officer in a number of different guises, irrespective of class, race, gender or age. Most importantly, they will vary in terms of the relationship to offending and the seriousness of the offending. Thus the scope will encompass the poor recidivist shoplifter, the well off drink driver, and the person committing serious assaults whose violence may be 'sparked' by excessive drinking.

The differing ways in which alcohol is used, viewed and responded to has significant implications for probation officers working in this area, as it is likely to influence some of the following issues:

■ how clients view their alcohol use,

■ how the probation officer perceives problem use and its related offending,

■ who defines whose problem it is, and who does what about it,

■ when intervention is and is not appropriate in this area,

■ the tension between client determination (of the problem) and the probation officer's concern about their re-offending.

❑ It's not a problem: whose problem and when?

Lance is seventeen. He has been placed on probation for an offence of assault on another youth committed outside a school. He has one previous conviction for theft. Whilst some concern was expressed at the nature of the more recent offence, it was seen by many (including Lance) as 'high jinks that got out of hand'. He was with a group of friends before the assault took place and they had been drinking in the pub beforehand. The court was concerned about the nature of this kind of incident, and Lance described very high levels of drinking to the probation officer preparing the PSR. Although Lance appeared very laconic and bored during the period of assessment, the probation officer felt that she had detected sufficient concern, and that there was at least tacit recognition from the client, that looking at his drinking may be useful to justify the recommendation for a probation order.

Phil is viewed by the team as a 'problem client'. When his case had to be re-allocated due to the departure of his previous PO, a mixture of groans and tell-tale glances emanated from the assembled team. When the newest officer agreed to take the case, he was met with a variety of well meaning and patronising comments. "Don't worry, Phil's OK really, and he'll be back inside soon in any case." "Phil's not too much trouble, it's his wife that is hard work – don't take any phone calls from her on a Friday afternoon".

Phil had, in fact, been known to this probation office for the last three years, mainly as a result of numerous offences of dishonesty. He was presently, according to the case file, enjoying a more stable period, and was back living with his wife and three children.

The probation officer taking on the above probation clients was very quickly faced with a number of questions and dilemmas:

1   Simply, to start with, were Phil and Lance drinking too much? By what criteria could this be judged? DSS Health Guidelines? Their physical condition? What they said? What their partners, friends or family said? The consequences of their offending, actions or lifestyle? Their history – often mapped out in numerous previous assessments and reports?

2   What if the probation officer picked up contradictory messages in relation to these? Would this indicate that the client was denying the extent to which their alcohol use may be causing problems? Would this indicate that the worker should push harder to intervene (for example, at the PSR stage) or rather that the client was not sufficiently motivated to begin to work on their problems? Or could such discrepancies indicate something else?

3   How would the probation officer begin to work with these apparently contradictory accounts and work out the different expectations and pressures from different people? What if there appeared a clear link between offending and drinking, yet the client denied this? Did this mean that the client could be offered nothing until their view (motivation) had changed? What if their view didn't change? Would this mean that the probation service would never offer them anything? What if the client initially accepted the need for probation, but once this had begun, maintained that alcohol was no longer problematic? To what extent did the probation officer have a responsibility to challenge this? In what way should this be done? If the client's drinking was not resulting in offending, and yet appeared to cause health problems or family difficulties, what right and or responsibility did the probation officer have to examine such problems?

❑ Definitions: what is normal drinking?

There are many phrases or concepts that attempt to describe patterns of drinking, and alongside these there are various 'safe guidelines', assessment techniques and questionnaires, which vary significantly in their complexity and sophistication. Some of these include:

- alcoholism,

- alcohol dependence syndrome (ADS),

- social drinking and controlled drinking.

The concept of **'alcoholism'** was very influential for some time and it was substantiated by the formation of Alcoholics Anonymous (AA) in the 1930s and the work of Jellinek (Jellinek 1960, as in Hunt 1982). Numerous studies by psychologists in the 1960s and 1970s – for example, the Rand Report 1976 (see for example McMurrin and Hollin 1993) – challenged the idea of problem drinking as a 'disease' and particularly the notion that a particular type of 'drinker' had only one hope of 'cure', namely abstinence. As a consequence, the 'disease model' of alcoholism has experienced a diminution in its influence, (particularly within helping agencies), whilst psychological models of drinking have gained strength, and 'controlled drinking' has become a more accepted goal. Thus cognitive-behavioural methods have assumed some considerable influence within the last decade (for example, see Davidson et al. 1991).

This is not to say, however, that the 'disease model' no longer has its supporters. Alcoholics Anonymous (with its related support groups Al-Anon, for the partners of problem drinkers and Alateen for their children) remains a large and valuable organisation, and many treatment centres and rehabilitation hostels operate the AA '12 Steps Approach' which emanate from such a model.

When looking through the case file on Phil, his new probation officer noticed a previous assessment that interpreted his drinking in such a light. It went like this:

> *Phil has had numerous periods of detoxification, and numerous, usually short spells in hospitals and rehabilitation centres. It seems clear that once he starts drinking he is unable to help himself. In this sense it appears that he has something of an addictive personality.*

Whilst the probation officer could understand that, in some senses, addiction is like a disease in that the poisonous effects of too much alcohol make Phil look and feel ill, particularly when he is suddenly deprived of it, she wondered whether it was helpful, in the long run, to regard the cause of his drinking as being, at least partly, out of his control. Might not this 'being done to' on his part, be unhelpful in terms of the potential for change; indeed, might it not be part of the very problem? In this sense the term 'alcoholism' may have unhelpful connotations and consequences:

> *... the idea of the 'disease' alcoholism suggests a medical problem, which ties into the whole range of beliefs concerning diseases and illnesses held in our society; treatment is the job of*

the medical profession; there is nothing I can do about my drinking – the solution is not my responsibility, it is the doctors'; and so on. (Vellman 1992)

Despite criticism of the disease model approach, there has been continuing research into the possible biological factors that may predispose individuals towards developing drinking problems (Valliant 1983; Cloninger 1987; Blum 1990) as in Barber (1995).

Whilst these are viewed as very controversial, as Barber (1995 *op. cit.*) observes:

Genetic advances are breathing new life into the disease notion of alcohol.

Because of the difficulties associated with the term, and its unhelpful tendency to label people, it was suggested by the World Health Organisation, in 1977, that the term 'alcoholism' be replaced by 'Alcohol Dependence Syndrome' (ADS). This more inclusive term involves looking at physiological, subjective and behavioural factors and may be seen as helpful (particularly by GPs) in assessing levels of alcohol misuse. The severity of the problem may be assessed by considering a number of clinically observable characteristics (Edwards 1977 in Hunt 1982). These include patterns of behaviour (for example, the extent to which an individual has narrowed the range of circumstances in which they drink and has developed a regular drinking schedule), subjective reactions (including drinking taking precedence over other activities and interests, thus affecting attitudes towards responsibilities and previously held values) and physical dependence (like an increase of tolerance towards alcohol, the type and extent of withdrawal symptoms in the absence of alcohol, for instance tremor, sweating, nausea, irritability, anxiety, and in more severe cases auditory and or visual hallucinations and withdrawal fits).

The probation officer taking over Phil's probation order felt that some of these concepts were useful. For example, it was helpful to look with Phil at certain periods in his past when he had become more and more centred on drinking to the exclusion of his family, and to try and consider in detail how and why this pattern had occurred. Furthemore, it made the probation officer consider the additional problems that psychological and physical dependence created for Phil at times when his drinking began to escalate. So, for example, Phil felt that feelings of failure as a father, led to feelings of depression and a tendency to drink more. Once excessive drinking had begun, he would recognise this and attempt to stop, but his withdrawal symptoms led to his behaviour becoming worse, thus leading to a vicious circle.

Those who accept the idea of an 'alcohol dependence syndrome' suggest that it takes account of the evidence challenging the existence of 'alcoholism', without denying the relevance of the medical contribution in dealing with alcohol related problems (particularly entrenched ones). Despite this, however, many would argue that ADS is still essentially a medical notion of a non-medical problem.

An additional problem with definitions that attempt to measure alcohol solely by the amount consumed or the effects of withdrawal, is that they tend to be somewhat blunt instruments in relation to the complex range of individuals who may have a particularly problematic relationship with alcohol. Many clients may not perceive a problem unless they see themselves somewhat stereotypically as 'an alcoholic'. 'Normal drinking' is a relative concept and many do not recognise a problem until it starts to escalate out of control. In fact, many do not acknowledge a problem even then, whilst the victims of their actions may have long been on the receiving end of the consequences. A good example of the disparity between the denial of alcohol's potential damage and its consequences is that illustrated by the 'drink driver', who may often voice a view that their average consumption of alcohol is 'below normal'. Alcohol is often a major contributory factor in committing other types of crime. It can be seen as a disinhibitor in relation to property crimes and offences of violence, including playing a role in domestic violence and child abuse cases.

Lance's probation officer struggled with these difficulties at the very start of contact. The CPS 'bundle' indicated that Lance had been highly intoxicated when arrested for the assault, which had involved punching and kicking another youth, who, fortunately, was not badly injured. Lance said that he had consumed about six pints of beer that evening, but did not consider that he was particularly drunk.

The probation officer attempting to make an assessment of Lance's drinking patterns at this initial stage of contact, felt that she was facing a number of confusing and often contradictory messages:

- Pressure from the magistrates to do something about this unruly youngster.
- A somewhat contradictory view from the solicitor that Lance's behaviour was both an isolated incident and a turning point!
- A nagging suspicion in her mind that Lance's behaviour might be like this most of the time.
- A young man in front of her who seemed bored, disinterested in the events happening around him and with no sense of the seriousness of what he'd done.
- Information from Lance's mother which suggested he hardly drank at all.

Amidst these somewhat contradictory voices, the assessment of Lance's drinking and its relation to his offending was no easy task. For, whilst the probation officer had acquired sufficient knowledge relating to safe drinking guidelines and was aware of the use of drinking diaries and other more sophisticated assessment questionnaires and techniques (see, for example, McMurrin and Hollin 1993), difficulties remained in relation to making sense of the picture, particularly concerning Lance's response. For, whilst he did, somewhat reluctantly admit that he occasionally went too far, generally he felt that his drinking (only really at weekends) and his behaviour (it was a fair fight) were in no way out of the ordinary. The problem was that Lance viewed such events in a different light from others, and the probation officer had somehow to make sense of Lance's response within the context of the other information that she was receiving.

In this sense, determining what constituted a 'drink problem' was less about judging Lance's alcohol intake or behaviour by some external set of criteria, (be that alcoholic, alcohol dependence syndrome, social or problem drinker) than about a process of 'negotiation' with Lance and others. This somewhat different way of attempting to define a drink problem was proposed by Vellman (1992):

> Whether or not someone has a drinking problem is not determined by fixed quantities of alcohol or fixed times, but is instead a matter of negotiation, by the individual with him or herself, family friends, work place and society as a whole.

By this definition, it is therefore legitimate for the probation officer to explore the problems (and potential problems) caused by reliance on alcohol as it affects the client, others in their life and the wider community. It is the offence, here, that legitimates such an exploration, although it should be stated such an exploration needs to be undertaken skilfully. Direct confrontation is unlikely to be effective due to the fact that, in this area of work, the client is likely to bring expectations of disapproval which may well further entrench feelings of defensiveness.

On reflection, the probation officer could see why that early period of assessment had proved so confusing and problematic. Not only had she been faced with the contradictory voices of those involved, but Lance's earlier responses had been influenced by events that it would have been impossible to reveal at that time.

Lance subsequently revealed that he had been drinking quite heavily at weekends (but not every weekend), mainly because he was bored, but wanted to get out of the house. There was significant marital conflict at home, and his father was, on occasion, physically violent towards his mother. Most significantly, his father had physically abused Lance during his early adolescence. It was extremely difficult to get Lance to talk about this, and there seemed to be a kind of conspiracy of silence with his mother.

Lance had thought of leaving home but was ambivalent for good reasons. He was bored at work with a somewhat dead end job and saw little prospects for his future. Weekend drinking was the norm with his friends and there were many disputes, arguments and some fights at these periods. Lance's violence on occasion had become particularly nasty and he was unable to account for the vehemence of his reactions, when he had been drinking. There was something about talking over his situation that he found useful, although his friends said that probation was a waste of time. His attitude towards his father switched from indifference to outright anger (in a sense, like his behaviour). Lance had some concern that he might end up like his uncle, who was viewed by the family as a 'boozer and waster'.

Seen within the context of this history, Lance's early response during the assessment period begins to make sense. Lance was unlikely to acknowledge more than he did at that time and that the assessment period was also a beginning of a process whereby Lance, with the probation office, was beginning, perhaps, to make links for the first time between the difficulties at home, his drinking, and his subsequent behaviour.

Whilst Lance's probation officer recognised that many of the tensions were inevitable, at the PSR stage, she felt that, on reflection, it might have been useful to bear in mind the following:

■ Clients will be affected by their anticipation of how information in relation to their drinking may be seen by the court when sentencing.

■ Clients and their solicitors may often wish to portray the present court appearance as a 'turning point'. Whilst the trauma of the court process may, on occasion, prove to be a significant motivating factor, there is always the danger that the client is presented as having reached a position that they have not, in fact, reached. Thus, there is a danger of setting them up to fail after the court appearance.

■ Knowledge of concepts of drinking, safe levels, and assessment questionnaires are important, but the worker needs to use these in conjunction with counselling skills to help the client make connections between their problems, drinking and offending, which are likely to be unique to every case.

■ The way in which drinking levels are assessed, or a history is taken, is important. It should be related to the client's circumstances, linking it with what you know about their situation – for instance, was last week a typical week? What was happening last week? Were you drinking more then? Why? Why not?

❑ Not hitting your head against a brick wall: the barriers to progress

If you thought that defining the extent of the problem, and whose problem it was, were thorny issues, wait till you get to developing ways of intervening, and helping clients stop or control their drinking.

A myriad of competing anxieties and pressures from the client, worker and agency can combine to leave the worker feeling drained and de-skilled. When goals are vague, expectations unrealistic and plans abandoned, workers and their clients can feel disillusioned. Workers, additionally, may feel increasingly reluctant to take on or work with such problems in a constructive way, faced with the complexities of interpreting what successful intervention would actually mean. Planned specific interventions and frameworks matched to the particular circumstances and characteristics of the client enable probation officers to recognise the real value of their work at different stages. Unless intervention is carefully planned on the basis of a thorough assessment and geared to the individual, proper evaluation of its effectiveness will be impossible. As Denney noted:

> *If probation officers are to have an opportunity of understanding the effects of their work, a serious effort must be made to assess the effects of their intervention. It is only when this process of evaluation is taken seriously by probation officers that discrimination in service delivery can be tackled. (Denney 1992)*

Before moving on to look at some approaches to methods of intervention, let us consider some of the obstacles which might be encountered. How such issues are or are not resolved will often determine the future success of specific interventions.

Carey was a 23 year old black woman, who had been remanded for a PSR. On receiving her appointment she had phoned the officer involved asking many questions about what the interview would involve, and why the matter had to be adjourned at all. At the first interview she seemed angry, and worried that her employers would find out about the offence. Whilst she accepted that driving with excess alcohol (about twice over the limit) was a serious offence, she stated that the circumstances at that time were unusual and that whilst she did drink socially, it was rarely, if ever to excess. The probation officer (a white man) felt that Carey did wish to talk to someone about the pressures in her life, and there were some discrepancies in relation to her account of her drinking. The court had indicated that a community sentence was the most lenient disposal that would be considered and a probation order was duly made.

The probation officer found the early stages of contact dominated by Carey's questions about the purpose and nature of the probation order, anger about the distance she had to travel to the office and frustration about having to sit in the waiting room before the appointment. It was difficult to begin to find a way to discuss Carey's drinking (let alone consider discussing ways to intervene) without this seeming confrontational, as she appeared increasingly defensive.

It was only after some time that Carey began to talk more freely about the pressures she was experiencing at work (her immediate manager would often engage in racist innuendo in the office) and at home (she had increasing financial responsibility for her parents). It became increasingly clear that such pressures had been accompanied by an escalation in her drinking, to a point where her controls of this were lessening. The worker was also becoming aware that Carey's initial suspicion, reticence and indeed anger were almost undoubtedly caused by her fears and expectations of what counselling in relation to her alcohol problems might mean, intensified by her personal experience as a black woman in a predominantly white society.

Carey faced some of the normal fears of such a process:

- fear of being judged,
- fear of being labelled,
- anxiety about what might be revealed about herself,
- fear of what change may entail.

Mixed in with these anxieties were other feelings relating to her experience as a black woman, such as being treated disparagingly within the dominant culture at work. Her contact with the criminal justice process in general and with the probation service in particular, added to her initial fears.

- Would this white, male probation officer abuse his position of authority?
- How would she be viewed by this agency?
- What experience did the probation service have of dealing with and understanding people from differing cultures and women?

- How did they deal with issues of racism and discrimination?
- Were most of the workers white?
- Were most of the clients white?

The probation officer was able to see, therefore, that Carey faced a number of barriers to contact which involved internal fears and anxieties, worries in relation to the agency, and anticipations influenced by her previous experience of discrimination. In addition, he had to examine his own attitudes to women who drink, and assumptions and stereotypes concerning women from Carey's particular culture and background. It was only by addressing these issues that the client and worker could move on to looking at the alcohol related difficulties in more depth and consider the different ways that the problems might be addressed.

In this case the client's feelings and expectations of the agency proved the initial barrier, but it is sometimes the case that the worker's attitudes and anxieties prove equally inhibiting. Thus the worker's fear of a particular type of client falling into this category or a particular type of behaviour (i.e. out of control) may significantly affect the worker's reaction, particularly their initial response.

People who have problems with drink (and more generally substance abuse problems) often attract stereotypical labels which can result in very powerful images of particular client groups which can be subtly pervasive of office culture and norms, often existing on the thresholds of office doors, and the edges of allocation meetings and supervision sessions. Shephard (1990) usefully identifies a number of common worker fears:

- a fear that the client will be manipulative and untruthful,
- a fear of violence,
- a fear that the client will attend in an intoxicated state,
- a fear that the client will make too many demands.

Such fears from the worker are not to be dismissed or precluded from the discussion. Indeed, some experience of the above may be true and it is necessary to explore such fears so that workers can respond more ably:

Stereotyping is a bigger issue in the substance misuse field than in most areas of work with other people. One reason for this is that most people dependent on substances lose much of the behaviour that is not associated with the substance use and become, in a sense, carica-tures of their former selves... They are easy to stereotype, and a convenient target for a society which seems to need a ready supply of folk-devils. However such an individual

75

resembles a negative stereotype of a substance misuser, and the helper should make the presumption in favour of that individual's desire for change, if they are asking for help. (Shephard 1990 op. cit.)

Whether or not most people actually become caricatures of their former selves is, we believe, questionable. It is important to remember that not every drinker fits a stereotype and equally important to bear in mind that drink problems come in many guises.

❑ Once a drinker, always a drinker? A positive approach to intervention

It should be becoming clearer at this stage that we are not proposing that methods of defining alcohol problems, assessing them and developing methods of intervening are separate processes. On the contrary, it can be seen that these often overlap. Thus assessment is not a single stage that happens prior to intervention, but rather the worker is making continuous assessments with the client in relation to the goal of effecting change. In the same way, exploring blocks to intervention is part of the intervention process itself, which will often need to be reconsidered or renegotiated.

This view of assessment and intervention as a changing process is particularly important in the area of alcohol problems and indeed other substance abuse difficulties. Partly this is due to the danger of stereotyping in this area of work which has just been discussed. However, additionally, the complex nature of addiction and the way in which people change in relation to this calls for a particular understanding that transcends the popular wisdom of becoming addicted, giving up or giving in.

There is a special need for workers to guard against the view of assessment as an established piece of knowledge, objectively true, collected and filed. Other writers in this field have pointed to the danger of extrapolating explanations of behaviour from such diagnostic assessments (Raynor 1985) and the strangling of effective intervention that can result. Preston-Shoot and Agass's comments seem even more relevant to this area of work:

There exists the illusion of the true, correct assessment. This omniscient fantasy and expectation, whilst comfortable for the public, threatens to disable practitioners, inhibiting and stultifying a process which can only be more or less useful and which must be creative and rigorous. (Preston-Shoot and Agass 1990)

It is important to avoid assessments becoming self-fulfilling labels whilst attempting to gain a perspective on the work that allows for different methods of intervention and levels of intervention at different 'stages' of difficulties.

This can be illustrated by the case of Phil. An excerpt from a previous sentence plan gives some of the flavour of a type of assessment that leads to an exhausting series of expectations and failures:

> Phil has a long history of drinking to excess when under pressure. Both his parents were heavy drinkers and he began to drink heavily himself following the breakdown of his first marriage. Drinking escalated to the point where he needed to fund this by means of shoplifting, particularly after losing his job. Phil's history suggests that he will be unable to control his drinking sufficiently to change his behaviour, at least in the short term. It may be worth trying another de-tox rehab., which seemed to have had some success in the past. His wife is becomingly increasingly frustrated and unable to cope. (December)

> Phil has made extremely encouraging progress in the last three months. Following his de-tox his drinking seems to have lessened. I think that his relationship with his wife has improved, and he seems less vulnerable to re-offending. Although he did not complete his stay at the re-hab, things, surprisingly, seem to have turned around. I discussed the case at Probation Liaison Committee and the magistrates were clearly impressed. (April)

> Phil has missed three of his last five appointments and I have written to him explaining that I will now probably have to breach him. His wife feels that he may be shoplifting again. He seems either unable or unwilling to sustain progress for any significant length of time… If he does come back to court on a breach it is going to be difficult to know what to say. (July)

Such assessments raise many questions and difficulties. What sense is made of Phil's previous drinking history? What is his view on why this has continued? In what ways is drinking affecting his life? What kind of steps has he taken previously to change the problem? To what extent does he consider it a problem? How does this fit in with his family's view? Why does he consider a de-tox at this time?

The 'process' of assessment and intervention means initially exploring with the client a number of factors in relation to their drinking and offending. These might include:

- Gaining an understanding of the client's knowledge of the risks and consequences of the drinking and offending behaviour.

- Gaining an understanding of the client's view of the problem.

- Gaining an understanding of the client's view of the stage they are at and how their drinking is affecting their lives.

- Exploring the client's prior and current coping mechanisms.

The process of 'choosing' and 'matching' interventions is then a development of the assessment process and not something that happens at the end of it. People's response to alcohol is likely to be forever changing in relation to the complex process of internal and external factors, and attempts therefore to objectify Phil's drinking behaviour are both unrealistic and can lead to over-optimistic aims and over-pessimistic conclusions.

❑ The cycle of change

Recent research into ways of understanding the change and decision making process has resulted in the development of useful frameworks which present a more detailed and realistic view of the complex stages that people experience in relation to dependencies. The best known of these – Prochaska and DiClementi's cycle of change (described in many books, for example Davidson et al. 1991) – provides a very valuable framework by which workers and clients can formulate more subtle, specific and realistic interventions. By showing that the client is experiencing different levels of motivation at different stages, Prochaska and DiClemente suggest the possibility of establishing the most appropriate type of intervention, or a combination of strategies for use at each stage of the client's relationship with alcohol (or indeed any addictive behaviour).

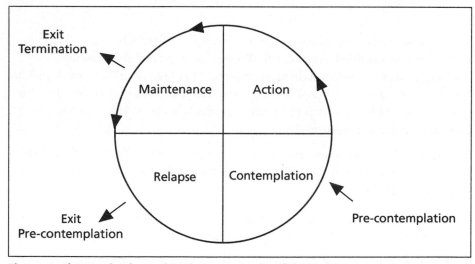

Figure 1 The Prochaska and DiClemente 'cycle of change'

The links between the stages of change and methods of intervention are illustrated by Fig.2

Stage and characteristics	Type of intervention considered
Pre-contemplation Clients at this stage may be unaware, or fail to acknowledge, that their drinking (or drug misuse) is causing problems. They may have been 'sent' by someone else (i.e. a partner or the court). They may be selective about the way they view negative consequences of their drinking (or drug misuse). They tend to think less about their behaviour and may do little to shift their attention away from the problem issue.	Engaging the client is of key importance. The way the client views the agency's response to the 'drinker' is very significant when motivation may be lacking (i.e. waiting time; attitude from secretarial staff; appointment letter). Methods indicated may be determined by the aims of encouraging a period of abstinence, change of drink, time spent thinking about drinking/drug-taking. Primary health care issues may be important (i.e. encouraging better nutrition). Additional considerations are the effect of their behaviour on children, parents, friends (e.g. see Tober 1991).
Contemplation Clients at this stage will start to recognise that something is wrong and begin to think about why. They may be troubled by the result of their actions without making a direct link with their behaviour (i.e. possible effect on their finances, relationships, court appearances). Despite some recognition the main characteristic is ambivalence about changing. It is often hard moving clients on from this stage.	A central aim of the worker is to shift the attitude of client to believing that losses associated with use outweigh the gains. Assessment techniques, feedback to client and educational groups (e.g. alcohol education groups) may be relevant, in addition to other methods encouraging client to move towards taking action. The techniques of 'motivational interviewing' are seen as particularly relevant at this stage.
Action Clients at this stage have made a decision to change and are attempting to find a way forward. The stage is analogous to the idea of reaching a 'turning point'.	A central aim of the worker is to help clients establish links between their drinking or drug misuse and the problems that have resulted. Methods used, therefore, are likely to include techniques enabling clients to formulate, specify and reduce the provoking problems (e.g. task centred case work; social skills; assertiveness training).
Maintenance Clients at this stage have made a sustained decision to stop. New habits are strengthened and clients practise new skills. The phase of 'staying stopped' is a crucial one that can be easily overlooked.	A central aim of the worker is to concentrate on possible difficulties of sustaining change (i.e. anticipating continuing or new pressures) and ways of replacing the misuse, given up with other activities.
Relapse Clients at this stage have experienced some setback – often as a result of a new crisis, negative self evaluation or poor self image.	The worker's attitude can be crucial in helping the client limit the setbacks and reinforce the progress made. There is an increasing body of literature dealing with techniques at this point (i.e. see 'relapse prevention for addictive behaviours').

Figure 2 How different stages in cycle of change indicate type of methods of intervention
(Adapted from ideas outlined by Prochaska and DiClemente (1984), and Davidson et al. (1991))

Prochaska and DiClemente's 'cycle of change' has become extremely influential as a framework for dealing with addiction problems – indeed it has been described as something of a bandwagon (Davidson in Barber 1995). It remains a valuable basis, we believe, for establishing types of intervention, if its limitations are borne in mind. Additionally, although it suggests that it is not aligned to any one theoretical school, it clearly has stronger ties and links with learning theories. Barber (op.cit.) interestingly suggests additions to the model that take into account the larger systems within which social workers and their clients have to operate.

In the case of Phil, for example, such a framework may have helped the client and worker move towards a plan of work something like this:

During our initial sessions we discussed the following:

1 Phil's feelings about being on probation for the third time. This reminds him of previous occasions when he has experienced a sense of failure by ending up before the courts; there are also issues in relation to the stigma attached to this and as it consequently effects his relationship with his wife, when he feels low and full of self-doubt. He acknowledges that, as a consequence, he has found it difficult to keep appointments with me, although he has done so. We have discussed the necessity of this in relation to the court order and Phil believes that this will get easier as the order progresses.

2 Phil's attitude towards the offence and his previous offending. So far it's early days in relation to this. On the one hand, Phil expresses tremendous guilt for his actions, particularly in relation to letting his family down. On the other hand, when he starts to 'binge drink' he appears to lose all sense of control until after the event (which, on the last two occasions, included stealing a quantity of alcohol from an off-licence). I believe we need to examine in some detail how and why such lapses occur.

3 Phil's history of drinking and his attitude towards drink now. We have discussed the fact that his view seems to switch from a complete determination to stop drinking, to heavy drinking periods. On one level, he sees himself as having no control; on the other hand, he feels that it's not so bad a problem as has been made out. My view is that Phil is at least ambivalent about drinking at the present time, and he acknowledges that a great deal of his life is centred around drinking. He does feel that in the past he has had most control over his drinking when he has had more responsibility in the household, and his relationship with his wife has improved as a result. He previously

found a local support group useful, but his experience of residential hostels has undermined his confidence.

4 Looking at issues of motivation, and how difficult it may be for him to cut down or stop at the moment, I think we are starting to acknowledge the differences between the way Phil is viewing the problem from the way others see it. Phil has said that when he "feels on the downward cycle his sense of control goes". He says that such periods start from perceived emotional pressures at home. It clearly is a stressful time, so we are devising ways in which such tensions can be managed by him to reduce the likelihood of further drinking and re-offending. I feel that Phil is very vulnerable. He is less than sure but acknowledges that past periods have often been mitigated by talking through his anxieties with friends, and seeking short-term medication for feelings of depression.

This formed the basis of Phil's supervision plan.

This plan would be less objective than the others, attempting to try and establish what stage Phil may be at in relation to change this time, and beginning to consider the positive and negative aspects of previous attempts to control drinking that may be built upon.

❑ Types of intervention

As clients experiencing alcohol problems come from a variety of different backgrounds and will be at different points in relation to their desire and ability to change, it is unlikely that one type of social work approach or method would be sufficiently flexible to deal with such a broad spectrum.

In considering different types of intervention, it is not only useful to keep in mind the framework in relation to change, but to consider particular aspects of the client's situation and drinking history in relation to this. For example:

- How does the drinking affect social aspects? Is the individual mainly drinking alone or with friends? Is this having an effect on relationships, children?

- What is the client's view of the pros and cons of giving up – abstinence or control?

- How does the client's age, background, cultural orientation and previous experience of authority affect their ability to accept intervention? Is this a young offender with poor educational experience or an older offender with a fear of groups?

- The client's perceived state of control over their drinking – are they, for example, in state of crisis?
- The severity of the problem – is there the necessity for medical intervention?
- The client's previous attempts to reduce or stop drinking. What has been successful? What are likely coping mechanisms?

Thus, for example, Phil may have presented himself at some stage to his probation officer in the following way:

Stating that he was drinking heavily, saying that he was helpless to do anything about it, expressing guilt, concerned about the effect of his behaviour on his family, unable to concentrate on dealing with one problem at a time, swamped with practical problems, unable to make a decision about drinking.

The probation officer would have felt that Phil's present circumstances represented probably at best an ambivalent attitude towards controlling his alcohol at this time (see the contemplation stage in Fig. 2). Intervention might be usefully targetted towards strategies which may enable him to manage the crisis period to minimise and or restrict the further escalation into drinking and the risk to re-offending.

Crisis intervention

So, in the first instance, the probation officer used some of the techniques developed from crisis intervention (Rapoport 1971; O'Hagan 1986) including:

- Allowing and enabling the client to express emotion, feeling, tension, so that a sense of autonomy can start to be regained.
- Allowing the client to work through feelings of disorientation, dislocation and helplessness so that they begin to regain coping mechanisms more quickly.
- Using the authority in the role of the PO appropriately by offering sufficient boundaries, while modelling confidence in relation to the client's ability to regain control.
- Using confidence and knowledge within the role in relation to the effects of alcohol.

In addition to this individual work, the probation officer considered negotiating meetings with Phil and his family to look at some useful damage limitation strategies if Phil's drinking continued.

Other methods may be more appropriate at different stages.

In the case of Carey, when some of the initial barriers had been worked through, the officer and client felt that it was important to look at some of the individual problems that were influencing her use of alcohol as an escape, and to try to effect quite specific change in these areas. The probation officer initially discussed whether such work was best undertaken by him, someone else in the agency or a referral on. They considered whether Carey would feel it necessary to gain support from some other individual or group more closely allied to her experience (including possibly challenging the legality of her boss's behaviour). They also looked at how she might respond to individual short-term counselling as opposed to a groupwork approach.

Short-term counselling

Short-term problem solving counselling involves:

- Looking at the essential problems – for example, the pressures at work leading to excessive drinking.
- Reorganising the problem to make it more resolvable – what steps could be taken to lessen her feelings of isolation or what remedies could be followed to challenge her manager's behaviour?
- Breaking down the problem into specific manageable steps.
- Working through blocks to achieving these.

Task centred work

These are some of the techniques that are outlined in task centred work (Reid and Epstein 1972; Doel and Marsh 1992).

In the case of Lance, it may have been felt that he would gain more from a situation which involved the provision of detailed information about alcohol, its effects on health, behaviour, and attitudes, within a group setting, which he might experience as less intensive than one to one counselling with an adult.

Alcohol Education Groups

These have, of course, been successfully run by most probation services for some time and they usually combine a mixture of information, discussion and participation, often using group processes – for example, peer group support or challenge – with exercises adapted from the field of education or psychology – the use of self assessment questionnaires, for instance. Such techniques are often particularly effective when used within such settings – drink diaries or 'craving' diaries are commonly used – and there has been much useful material developed in relation to relapse prevention (see, for example, Wanigaratne et al. 1990). Such techniques can also be adapted for individual use.

Lance found the group experience difficult at first, but seemed to gain a lot from the support of other group members as it progressed, and as a consequence appeared to be less defensive about the extent of his drinking and the pressures on him to continue this. In fact, he found the ending of the group and the transition back to one to one contact difficult.

Whilst this form of intervention has often proved to have been particularly effective, consideration always needs to be given to how the group programme and work undertaken there fits in with the overall probation order. In relation to clients attending such programmes conditionally as part of a probation order or unconditionally, it is useful to be aware of some of the following issues:

- The importance of purposeful three-way meetings between the client, the officer responsible for the order and the group leaders.
- The importance of establishing progress and what has yet to be achieved – the client may have attended unfailingly, but if there is a perceived need for further work to be done following the group, how is this negotiated?
- Do the group workers and individual PO have different expectations or perceptions of progress made?
- Does the programme represent the main part of the order or only part of the order?

We have stressed that working with alcohol problems involves using skills in relation to defining and negotiating the problem, assessing the problem and intervening, but that these processes are not discrete. In particular, we have stressed that this type of work involves dealing with people at very different stages of difficulty, and the consequent need to develop strategies that take into account such differences so that energies can be directed positively and effectively. With hindsight, it can often be seen that the most apparently intractable situations in relation to alcohol dependence have changed through the perseverance of the worker at the most traumatic time. We believe it is vital for probation officers to acknowledge the effectiveness of such intervention in relation to their clients' lives and their clients' offending.

Cue Orchestra!

REFERENCES

1. Barber, J. (1995) *Social Work with Addictions*, London: Macmillan

2. Davidson, R., Rollnick, S. and MacEwan, I. (1991) *Counselling Problem Drinkers*, London: Tavistock/Routledge

3. Denney, D. (1992) *Racism and Anti-Racism in Probation*, London: Routledge

4. Doel, M. and Marsh, P. (1992) *Task Centred Social Work*, Aldershot, Ashgate

5. Hunt, L. (1982) *Alcohol Related Problems*, London: Heinemann

6. McMurrin, M. and Hollin, C. (1993) *Young Offenders and Alcohol Related Crime*, London: Wiley

7. O'Hagan, K. P. (1986) *Crisis Intervention Social Services*, London: Macmillan

8. Preston-Shoot, M. and Agass, D. (1990) *Making Sense of Social Work*, Hampshire: Macmillan

9. Rapoport, L. (1971) 'Crisis Intervention as a Mode of Brief Treatment', in R. W. Roberts and R. H. Nee (eds.) *Comparative Theories in Social Casework*, University of Chicago Press

10. Raynor, P. (1985) *Social Work Justice and Control*, London: Whiting and Birch

11. Reid, W. J. and Epstein, L. (1972) *Task Centred Casework*, New York: Columbia University Press

12. Shephard, A. (1990) *Substance Dependency; A Professional Guide*, Birmingham: Venture Press

13. Vellman, R. (1992) *Counselling for Alcohol Problems*, London: Sage

14. Wanigaratne, S., Wallace, W., Pullin, J., Keaney, F. and Farmer, R. (1990) *Relapse Prevention for Addictive Behaviours*, Blackwell Scientific Publications

6
Working with sex offenders

People who commit sexual offences are the subject of much debate, both in general, and in probation circles (Scully 1990; Dominelli 1991; McColl and Hargreaves 1993; Home Office 1993; Sampson 1993; Brown 1994). Here we have perhaps one of the most difficult and controversial areas of work where arguments about methods of intervention, treatment, approaches and appropriate disposal rage, and where the personal and the professional are often in conflict. The probation service's commitment and brief to provide community resources for sex offenders, as well as joint prison/probation initiatives for working with sex offenders during their sentences are the subject of much discussion (Sampson 1993; Brown 1994). Here, as elsewhere, we must do battle with stereotypes, fantasies and what is often the most difficult and unacceptable in human behaviour. The implications for working with difference in this context are considerable.

The area of sexual offences is also unusual because it is probably the only one in which the conduct of the victim is frequently under as much scrutiny as the conduct of the offender. If your house is burgled, you are not challenged about the amount of property you possess, your security arrangements, the untidiness of your cupboards... if your car is stolen, you were not, until recently, rebuked for having a car in the first place. If you are the victim of a sexual offence, however, where there is a not guilty plea, you can find yourself as much on trial as the perpetrator.

Working with this client group is fraught with all kinds of complex problems and questions. What do sex offenders look like? Is this only the domain of men? What about the small group of women who sexually abuse? There is a plethora of practice dilemmas thrown up by the feelings evoked. How can we hold the actual victims in our minds whilst acknowledging and working with the victim in the victimiser? How do we reconcile this with the assessment of risk? As Mark (1992) observes, probation officers rarely ever feel ready or equipped for this type of work.

Working with sex offenders is an area about which it is almost impossible to be unmoved. What do we think about such people? Indeed what do we mean when we say 'such people'? After all, there is a range of types of sexual offence, with different motivations and aetiologies.

The first problem, as Sampson (1994) points out, is to answer the question "What do we mean by a sexual offence?" This turns out to be a difficult question to answer in many respects as the law relating to sexual behaviour is often confused. Rape within marriage, sado-masochism, consensual buggery between males and between a man and a woman have all been the subject of debate and changes in views and opinions. This raises the question of how far we should broaden or narrow our definition of which aspects of sexual conduct should be labelled crimes. Sampson offers this useful definition of a sexual crime:

> There is a basic distinction that can be drawn between sex which is deviant or illegal and sexual abuse, between behaviour which produces victims and behaviour which does not. Unless a sexual act is freely entered into with full, informed consent, or if its consequences are seriously harmful, then, it can be argued, it should be classified as a sexual crime. (Sampson 1994, pp. 4-5)

In this chapter, then, we are going to focus on behaviour which produces victims, where informed consent is absent and where the consequences of such actions are harmful. Alongside this, we will examine the issues presented by people who commit the kind of serious sexual offences that are likely to earn them either community sentences with a high restriction of liberty or prison sentences, and the dilemmas that they pose. These are people who are a risk to the public and require careful assessment and monitoring. The emphasis will be on predatory rather than consensual behaviour, irrespective of the fact that, as we have already suggested, the law still defines some actions which fall into the latter category as illegal. As O'Callaghan and Print point out "interpersonal sexual behaviour which does not involve mutually consenting participants is abusive " (in Morrison et al. eds. 1994, p. 147).

❏ What is sex offending all about?

This is a question with many different possible answers. Sex offending is often about power, control, and assumptions about what men should be and what women and children are for. It can also be about fantasies to do with sexuality, sexual inadequacy and immaturity, inability to make relationships or inability to deal with some of the powerful emotions which relationships generate. Offenders may seek to punish or exact revenge, to generate fear, to provoke excitement. Whatever the reasons, and however little violence is employed, it is usually an angry, violent act.

There is a range of theories about the roots and causes of sexual offending and these have had obvious implications for methods of intervention – to which we will return later in the chapter. First let us consider some of these theories and the related treatment approaches.

Biological perspectives

These rest on assump ions about sex drives – in particular innate high sex drives in certain men which feed into popular myths about 'uncontrollable beasts', 'insatiable appetites' and so on. Some of these assumptions may be seen to be reflected in the more controversial court judgments which appear sympathetic to the sexual needs of men which nature dictates must be satisfied – sometimes at all costs!

The theory is that some men have abnormal sex drives, often linked to sexual aggression, which lead to uncontrolled sexual behaviour. The solution is often seen to be via drug therapy, or more dramatically and controversially, through surgery. Overall such views are seen to represent a rather one dimensional view of sexual offending, raising both ethical dilemmas and questions about the effectiveness of treatment.

Learning theories

As we saw in Chapter 3, learning theories rest on the assumption that all behaviour is learned. In theory, then, sex offenders learn to be aroused by inappropriate stimuli and this behaviour is reinforced by lack of punishment or by the fact that someone influential in the individual's life is behaving in the same way. Thus, for example, a sexually abused child may be presented with a model of sexual behaviour that becomes a normal way of life. This in turn affects the way the individual thinks about both their own sexuality and sexuality in general – a set of ideas about this is then developed to justify and reinforce the behaviour.

Here the solution would be to change the individual's thinking by challenging the distortions and assumptions which lie behind the behaviour on the basis that if you can change the way people think, you can change the way they act. Techniques for challenging offenders' thinking in this way often form a large part of group work approaches currently used in the probation service and in prisons.

Socio-cultural theories

These embrace feminist perspectives and focus on the power imbalances between men and women and between adults and children. Such theories rest on assumptions about the socialisation of men and women – the former being encouraged to be powerful and superior and the latter to be submissive and subordinate. Thus sexual offending is a manifestation of men's attempts to maintain power over women and keep them in a subordinate role, or to exert power and superiority over someone – a child – clearly far less powerful than themselves. Some feminist accounts, in contrast to other theories, do not distinguish sexual offending from normal relations between men and women, but view it as the extreme end of a continuum of behaviours which reward men by exploiting women.

Here approaches would inevitably focus on issues of power, powerlessness and assumptions about the relationships between men and women and men and children.

Psychodynamic theories

These present the sex offender as basically unfulfilled and suffering from extreme interpersonal conflicts. These are usually seen to have their roots in unresolved childhood struggles, notably surrounding the coming to terms with relationships with either parent. This, it is argued, can lead to regressed behaviour (individuals may seek out child victims and treat them as they wish they had been treated) or behaviour aimed at symbolic revenge; rapists may be seen to be experiencing powerful mixed feelings towards their mothers. Sexual offences are also seen as a search for power and control in order to conquer childhood trauma.

Approaches, in this framework, need to include a psychodynamic exploration of the offender's own victimisation and its meaning for their childhood – in other words, intervention would need to address both the child and the adult within the individual.

❑ Types of sexual offence

The sexual abuse of children

This is the sexual gratification of an adult by using a child. Studies indicate that between 80 and 95 per cent of the adults concerned are male, and that the victims are usually female (Jennings 1993; Waterhouse et al. 1994). The issue of female sex offending has been largely ignored until fairly recently (Elliott 1993). We will look at this area in a moment.

Finklehor's (1987) four pre-conditions, which are met prior to the perpetrator committing sexual abuse, emphasise how motivation is established and how internal inhibitions and external impediments are overcome. Although he was writing about child sex offenders, his suggestion of a sequence of four pre-conditions, is usually seen to be applicable to most sex offenders.

1 The potential offender needs to have some motivation to sexually abuse a child.

2 A potential offender has to overcome internal inhibitions against acting on that motivation.

3 A potential offender has to overcome external impediments to committing sexual offences.

4 A potential offender has to undermine or overcome a child's resistance to the sexual offence.

All this takes an investment of time and energy on the part of the perpetrator, and consequently such behaviour is unlikely to be easily stopped or controlled.

Victims of sexual abuse can be as young as 12 months old and both the short and the long-term effects upon them can be devastating. A recent study, carried out for the Scottish Office by Edinburgh and Cardiff Universities (Waterhouse et al. *op. cit.*) discovered that 77 per cent of the abused children who were the victims of the offenders in their sample were under 12 years old at the time the abuse began, 75 per cent were girls and most of the abusers were either the father, stepfather or another male relative. The authors of the study drew particular attention to the level of aggression involved towards the children – in half the cases physical violence or coercion was used.

Probation officers will often encounter clients for whom the experience of childhood abuse proves to be a significant factor in their offending behaviour, and whose lives have been blighted and contaminated by the feelings of guilt and self-loathing that childhood sexual abuse can engender.

Sexual abuse can take place both within and outside the family and most abusers are heterosexual males who are known to the child, and in a position of trust and authority. Sexual abuse is often about jealousy, anger, resentment and power. Abusers will often explain their behaviour by blaming someone or something else – a frigid or pregnant partner, a seductive child who 'led them on' (remember the child who was described by Judge Ian Starforth Hill as "not entirely an angel herself" at the ripe old age of eight?), the influence of alcohol, drugs, or some kind of trauma. Here we identify and describe two kinds of child sexual offence, which reflect some of the elements we have just described.

Paedophilia

This means literally the sexual love of children. Here the individual has an obsessive fixation in relation to children, often strongly identifying with them. The forming of sexual relationships with children may be connected to a failure to achieve a satisfactory adult sexual relationship, with the associated connotation of having failed as a man. The backgrounds of paedophiles are often disturbed. Paedophilia is sometimes related to feelings of nostalgia and sadness for a childhood now lost and the person concerned may prefer to think of themselves as a fellow child in the relationship rather than an adult. Within this relationship, the child is seen to provide affection without strings, as well as enabling the perpetrator to gain a sense of power and superiority. The most common type of behaviour is sexually interfering with children rather than actually having intercourse. Research suggests that offenders commit far more offences than they are actually charged with and that these may only represent the tip of the iceberg. The most significant self-report study in recent years proposed that paedophiles who targetted boys committed on average 282 offences, involving a total of 20 victims each. (Abel et al. 1987).

Wyre (1987) identifies two kinds of paedophile – the fixated paedophile and the regressed paedophile. In the case of the **fixated paedophile**, the individual experiences no sexual arousal with adults, is much more comfortable with children and is likely to have been sexually abused himself as a child. Access to children could well be part and parcel of the working environment; the perpetrator may work with children or be in a position of trust in relation to them. The child victim will be seduced over time with bribes and threats and will also be made to feel partly responsible for the sexual relationship that develops.

The **regressed paedophile**, in contrast, is attracted to women and may be in a stable relationship. He is likely to molest a child impulsively in response to a crisis and although may feel shame as a consequence, may easily repeat the behaviour. Wyre (*op. cit.*) suggests that many paedophiles get described in this way by sentencers due to over sympathetic pre-sentence reports.

Incest

We thought it was useful to consider this as a separate category since a different type of dynamic applies. Incest breaks a fundamental taboo. Within the safety of the family, which has as its cornerstone the trust between parent and child, relationships are established based on fear, mistrust and the abuse of power. There is also no escape – the victim is in constant contact with the abuser. The most usual perpetrators of incest are step-fathers, and biological fathers although brother/sister incest is not uncommon and there is a small minority of women who have also committed incest (more about this later). Incest is usually shrouded in secrecy and relies on threats – "mummy will leave us if you tell anybody " or, "you'll be taken away". The child is also made to feel responsible for what has happened and the mother will often be either seen to have colluded with the behaviour or to have failed to protect the child. Familial incest offenders appear to be the least recidivist. (Abel et al. *op. cit.*)

Female sexual abuse of children

The whole area of women and sexual abuse is relatively uncharted territory. It has only been since the late 1980s that studies in this area have emerged (Jennings *op. cit.*) so research is at an early stage. Current statistics however indicate that 5 per cent of abused girls and 20 per cent of abused boys were the victims of women (Finkelhor and Russell 1984). As probation officers we are unlikely to come across female sex offenders because prosecution is rare. This is because victims of female abusers find it even more difficult to tell anyone about what has happened and are even less likely to be believed (Elliott *op. cit.*). We do, however, need to know something about this area so that we can retain actively listening and well informed ears when clients tell us what may seem like an extraordinary story, and so that we may resist the urge to make assumptions and to stereotype people on the basis of gender. After all, people found it hard to believe that the physical abuse of children took place once upon a time and look where we are now....

As the title of Elliott's book affirms, female sexual abuse is 'the ultimate taboo'. It is more threatening because it cuts at the deepest roots of our assumptions about how women should relate to children, and it also challenges some of the theories we have already highlighted in terms of the role that child abuse plays in the context of male power and aggression. Women are not supposed to be sexually aggressive, according to the theory, and any inappropriate sexual behaviour towards children is perceived as the result of male coercion. Research now indicates that coercion was rarely present in the majority of instances (Kinder Mathews in Elliott 1993). We are far more ready to believe in male abuse, too. We assume that women are not capable of it because they do not have penises, forgetting all the ways in which children can be used sexually for adult gratification. Unfortunately, however shock proof we think we have become, there may still be some kinds of behaviour that will stop us in our tracks.

Exhibitionism ('flashers')

This is about rage and power – the idea is to frighten, shock and triumph. Excitement for the perpetrator is heightened by risk – the offender often does not run away. Accounts are often plausible – "it was an accident", "I didn't realise". One of us (who shall remain nameless) was completely taken in, as a first year officer, by the convincing tale of the young man who was applying ointment to his penis in front of an open window, as it was such a lovely day, not realising he could be seen by every passer by....

Exhibitionism may be seen to be linked with experiences of victimisation as a child including, an over-dependence on mother or a dominant mother and a distant relationship with the father. The behaviour is seen to contain a wish to punish the family, as well as the desire for power and the need to triumph by frightening or shocking someone else.

Rape

Once again we turn to Wyre (*op. cit.*) who usefully defines four different types of rape, each with slightly different characteristics and emphasis. We found these particularly helpful in relation to assessment in general and risk assessment in particular. The four types he identifies are:

- sexual rapists
- anger rapists
- sociopathic rapists
- sadistic rapists.

Abel et al. found that rapists tended to be younger than other sex offenders and averaged seven offences per conviction.

Sexual rape

Sexual rapists are characterised by their problems in relationships with women, and what can be seen as a passive/submissive personality. Such individuals are often very preoccupied with what they see – or more painfully what has been pointed out to them – as their own sexual inadequacy, and have a poor self image. They satisfy their sexual urge by attacking and raping women, although they will use minimal violence to achieve their end and are likely to back off if challenged. Their approach tends to be a sudden grab, in the hope that the victim will submit easily.

People who fall into the 'sexual rapist' category usually have a history of petty sexual offences (obscene phone calls, indecent exposure, frottage – rubbing up against people in crowded places, like the underground). They may often have been abused or bullied as youngsters.

Anger rape

The anger rapist according to Wyre (*op. cit.*) usually has a woman in his life who he sees as dominant and who he fears and resents. Such an individual often holds extreme images of womanhood in his mind – she is either Madonna (in the biblical rather than rock star sense) or whore; worthy of being placed on a pedestal or treacherous and demanding. The anger rapist often employs a 'macho' style, and can be possessive and prone to jealousy. His sense of his masculinity, ironically, is very fragile and he will react violently and dramatically if this is called into question, even in jest.

Anger rape is about domination, degradation and control. It involves weapons, unnecessary violence – that is, violence above and beyond what might be needed to terrify and subdue the victim – and threats of mutilation or death. The anger rapist attacks strangers, close to home usually, in response to a relationship problem. Charm and chat may be employed whilst awaiting the opportunity to attack.

Sociopathic rape

Rapists in this category don't see themselves as sexual offenders – they are primarily criminal or anti-social and their approach to women is just part of what they see as normal behaviour. Often charming and plausible, their thinking is dominated by typical sexist attitudes about what women are 'really' there for, what they really mean when they say "no" and so forth. Often the rape is opportunist – that is to say done in the course of another anti-social act, like burglary, just because a woman happens to be there. The perpetrator will use minimal violence – he does not want to be caught – but uses threats of violence aimed at getting women to go through the motions of normal love making – kissing, undressing etc.. This makes court proceedings tricky as the victim is often perceived as being a willing participant....

Sadistic rape

Extremely dangerous and fortunately quite rare, this is the action of someone who is generally emotionally and mentally disturbed. Sadistic rapists are excited by pain and fear – and even the prospect of the death of the victim – and will launch a cold blooded attack, often using weapons and threatening or carrying out acts of mutilation. Individuals who commit this kind of offence tend to be over controlling or obsessive. They may be people in the grip of some kind of reforming zeal or religious belief which involves punishing women, on the basis that they lead men into sin. Perhaps the most famous example of the sadistic rapist is The Yorkshire Ripper, who exhibited all the characteristics just described, and whose sexual attacks ended in the deaths of most of his victims.

Indecent assault

Indecent assault covers a wide range of types of behaviour from frottage, referred to earlier, and 'bottom pinching' to forced oral sex and sexual molestation. Such offences, though they may be thought of as less serious by some, still cause terror and a sense of degradation and revulsion in the victim.

Unlawful Sexual Intercourse (USI)

It is an offence for a male to have sexual intercourse with a girl under 16. If she is under 13 the penalties tend to be more severe (Gilyeat 1994). Probation officers may encounter this offence in various forms. Often both parties are very young and it is parents or other adults who insist on prosecution. The other typical scenario is where the male partner is significantly older and more mature and the law takes the view that advantage has been taken of the young woman's vulnerability. USI is quite tricky since both partners are often in a long standing relationship, and assessments have to be made on that basis.

Sexually related offences

There are certain kinds of behaviour that might not appear serious on the surface, but could be the precursor of more serious sexual behaviour in the future. Obviously, it is dangerous to make too many assumptions on this basis, but your warning bells could usefully be tweaked if you encounter people who have voyeuristic tendencies – watching people undress, frequenting lovers' lanes minus lover, peeping over walls in public lavatories – or who do things like stealing underwear from clothes-lines, or making obscene phone calls.

Very much more serious – and useful to consider – is the offence of arson, in this context. Arson is of course an offence in its own right. What is worth considering though, for the purposes of both risk assessment and appropriate intervention, is the links that have been made between arson and sexual/ sensual pleasure and between arson and evidence of sexual difficulties (Prins 1986). Although at one time there was a great stress on the relationship between sexual activity and fire raising – a nineteenth century German theory which received support from both Freud and Jung – modern writers see sexual factors as only part of the story but nonetheless worth taking into account. Psychosexual and marital problems, problems in forming social relationships with women and sexual disorders have all been found in a proportion of men convicted of arson (Hurley and Monahan 1969). Awareness of these links could prove helpful, both in considering avenues of exploration at the PSR stage, and appropriate forms of disposal.

❑ Children and sex offending

The notion of children as sexual offenders is, unfortunately, no longer as shocking as it once was. Recent reports in the press of young adolescents convicted of sexual offences cause us to ponder on how and why such behaviour is now emerging. We probably all remember the case of the 15 year old convicted of rape who was ordered to pay his victim £500 so she "could have a jolly good holiday". Startling as it may seem, Home Office Statistics for 1990 covering sexual offences reported in 1989 show that out of 10,729 people found guilty or cautioned for such crimes, 20 per cent were 17-20, 9 per cent were 14-16 and 3 per cent were 10-13.

As probation officers you are unlikely to encounter very young people charged with such a crime, but you may encounter older adolescents charged with sexual offences, and you will be working with young people whose exposure to sexual abuse may have led them to behave in this way to others.

Research both in the USA and in this country suggests that juvenile sexual offending must be taken seriously and that specialist intervention should be provided as soon as possible. Just because the perpetrators are young, the impact upon the victim is no less great and what are referred to as 'hands off' offences – frottage, voyeurism, obscene phone calls – have the potential to become 'hands on' offences involving sexual assault. As Richardson (1990) observes, unlike other kinds of juvenile offending, where the young person is likely to grow out of the behaviour, by virtue of the simple passage of time, the same is not true of sexual offending. The dangers inherent in explaining away unusual sexual behaviour as experimentation, getting carried away, sowing wild oats etc. are obvious when viewed in this context. Abel et al.

97

(*op.cit.*) identified the onset of sexually deviant behaviour at an early stage in many offenders.

Richardson (*op.cit.*) emphasises the knowledge and skills which are prerequisites for good practice when working with adolescent abusers. Crucial to any kind of intervention is an awareness of relevant theory in relation to the psychosexual development of adolescents – or as O'Callagan and Print (1994) put it, an ability to distinguish normal adolescent sexual behaviour, and therefore identify what might be termed 'worrying' sexual behaviour which should cause the old alarm bells to ring.

Normal behaviour might include explicit sexual discussion, obscene jokes, masturbation, use of erotic material, innuendo, flirtation and consensual sexual activity. Behaviour that should sound alarm bells and suggests assessment or intervention is required includes compulsive masturbation, use of violent pornographic material, sexually explicit conversations with much younger people, sexually explicit threats, forced sexual contact, persistent obscene phone calls, exhibitionism or frottage.

The skills required are very much a reflection of those employed with adult perpetrators, to be discussed later on in this chapter. A family work approach can be very helpful with young sexual offenders as family functioning may be relevant to the behaviour exhibited.

What about the characteristics of juvenile sex offenders? Here again we enter difficult territory since many of the identified factors could be just as true for young people engaging in non-sexual crime. These include poor social skills, inability to make and sustain friendships with people of the same age, difficulties in asserting themselves and controlling anger. Many young child abusers were found to be socially isolated, anxious and depressed, with a poor sense of self-esteem and a tendency towards suicidal ideas and behaviour (O'Callaghan and Print, *op.cit.*). Experiences of being bullied also appeared to be a characteristic of this group. Here we see there are more similarities between young sex offenders and young offenders in general than there are differences.

Becker and Kaplan (1988), however, found that young sex offenders, in contrast to other offenders, had no previous criminal history, were less likely to be violent or abuse substances – characteristics born out by research undertaken by O'Callaghan and Print in Manchester. Family chracteristics have also been studied (by Smith and Israel 1987), who suggest that young sex offenders are likely to come from families where the parents are distant and inaccessible, where a sexual climate is encouraged and where there is a family history of maintaining secrets.

❑ Issues for practice

Simon and Maurice, whose histories now follow, exemplify many of the personal and the professional tensions that face probation officers working with sex offenders.

Simon is aged 24 years and has been remanded in custody charged with three offences of indecent assault. He is asking for two others to be taken into consideration. The offences took place over a two week period in a park near to where he works in the post room of a large company and involve his touching women walking past – on the bottom, breasts and between the legs. On one occasion he went back and pinched the woman again, grinning and inquiring whether she would like to see his penis. He has a previous conviction for a similar offence earlier this year and prior to that several for indecent exposure dating back four years.

Following the separation of his parents soon after he was born, Simon, the youngest of three children, lived with his mother until he was six. He was then taken into care because she abused him physically. Periodically he was returned to her, but things would deteriorate after a while and he would go back into care. When he was 15 his father made contact and he went to live with him for a year, but his father then left to live with another woman and the contact was lost once again.

Maurice is a 38 year old man who is due to be released on licence in three months time. He will have served over five years of an eight year sentence for offences of rape and indecent assault. These offences were committed against a 12 year old girl who had been a friend of the family. Maurice had been married for some two years before the commission of the offences. His wife had a breakdown some months after the trial and they have now separated. They have no children.

During his childhood Maurice moved constantly between one parent and another due to their constant rows, arguments and violence. He experienced severe physical abuse which took particularly degrading forms. When he was 13 he was taken into care and spent two and a half years in a children's home, about which he speaks little. Following this, he went to live with his aunt, appeared to make significant progress at a local secondary school, and eventually developed a successful career as an accountant.

He pleaded not guilty to the charges and, following his conviction, made an unsuccessful appeal. He has one previous conviction for indecent assault, ten years ago for which he received a suspended sentence.

Risk Assessment

Assessing risk is, of course, one of the main issues in this area. Whilst all sex offenders do not have common characteristics, as we have seen, the level and extent of their aggression, feelings of inadequacy or capacity to change will always be central matters of concern for probation staff proposing and implementing methods of intervention. The high risk nature of the offending or potential offending determines to an extent methods of assessment and the particular emphasis of types of intervention.

Assessing risk is a continuing facet of work with sex offenders and needs to be undertaken at every significant stage of contact or potential change of contact or circumstances. (See Chapter 2 'Risk and dangerousness' for more general comments).

Making an initial assessment is, however, a particularly crucial time as the way in which issues of the seriousness of the current offence, offending history, denial and confrontation are dealt with at this time may determine how future contact will proceed. As was observed by the HM Inspectorate of Probation in their report on the work of the probation service with sex offenders (1991):

> *If a report writer had colluded with the offender at this stage in avoiding or minimising the offence, or the history of offending behaviour, essential confrontation at any subsequent stage of supervision was likely to prove more difficult.*

PSR preparation often represents the cutting edge for probation officers in this type of work. Thus, the probation officer preparing the report on Simon faces a number of emotional and professional challenges.

Along with her other work, initially at least, this represented one more PSR to be completed by a relatively short deadline. Simon was in custody, and although it would be difficult visiting twice, she realised that this would be essential if she were to make a thorough assessment. On looking at the CPS bundle, she was unsettled and troubled by the details of his offending, feeling that a custodial sentence, was in any event perhaps the most suitable and likely outcome. Such feelings are both understandable and often appropriate. Feelings of fear, disgust or anger may be evoked and and workers may think that they just do not want to sit in the same room and have to discuss the detail of such behaviour.

It is important to recognise the impact that such feelings will have upon the worker which can induce a number of different responses. Both male as well as female officers can often feel violated and paralysed by an encounter with an offender who may have committed a particularly heinous crime. In what

Jean Moore (1990) describes as the "penetration of professional distance", the actual worker herself becomes, in a sense, another victim. To counter this, Moore stresses the importance of establishing and maintaining the distance of the professional role. Female workers are more likely to experience physical unease and possible threat in addition to this emotional unease, and it is vital that any identified response is immediately listened to and appropriate action and support implemented.

An alternative response may involve an over-identification with the victim part of the abuser. This happened, to an extent, to the probation officer preparing a report on Simon. Whilst initially very disturbed by the details of his offences, her empathic recognition of the pattern of Simon's own history of abuse at the hands of his mother, may have led her to lose some overall focus. As a result there could be a danger of overidentifying with the victim in the victimiser and losing a sense of the real victims of the offence. She could easily have been seduced by Simon into believing that she had managed to understand and make an impact on him, where others had failed.

Another response may be to launch headlong into an overtly hostile confrontational approach as a response to the anger evoked by the offender's crimes and apparent lack of acceptance and remorse etc.. Whilst this is understandable, it should be kept in mind that the aim of intervention is most effectively and systematically to challenge behaviour that puts victims at risk and this involves engagement of the offender as well as effective confrontation.

As we have seen, work with sex offenders evokes extremely powerful emotions and responses in professionals. It is important that such feelings are recognised, thought through and discussed in supervision and with relevant colleagues. They are often a clue to what the offender is experiencing and offer valuable insights into motivation, and risk of re-offending. Most significantly, if workers are to continue to work effectively, they need to be supported in making sense of the feelings evoked, so these can be dealt with and not spill over into their personal lives.

As the emotional response is likely to prove so significant for workers, the importance of consultation through the assessment process cannot be overestimated. Time spent at this stage is worth its weight in gold in helping the worker establish a proper assessment of risk and professional intervention.

The probation officer preparing the report found it initially difficult to provide a professional service to Simon whilst keeping in mind the overriding responsibility to the victim and potential future victims of his actions. This involved acknowledging that the client had probably been through this process before, that the aim of the assessment was to help make sense of why such offences had been committed, and to outline the limits of confidentiality i.e. that new offences coming to light would be reported.

Simon appeared highly embarrassed about having to talk about himself. He appeared withdrawn and depressed and initially stated that he had only pleaded guilty to the three offences of indecent assault through the persuasion of his solicitor. The probation officer had to adopt a sceptical and challenging attitude towards Simon's account whilst avoiding confrontation for confrontation's sake (we will return to issues of denial and confrontation a little later). After a time, Simon had admitted to her some level of sexual offending. He had related this to feelings of anger and frustration at a time when he was being made fun of at work. However, he admitted similar feelings prior to his last offence and, whilst the probation officer identified some potential encouragement in his willingness to discuss such feelings, she also felt that his progression from indecent exposure to indecent assault represented a dangerous development. In view of what he had suffered at the hands of his mother, there are fears that his acutely hostile attitude towards women may escalate further into more serious offences against women.

Thus, whilst the PO's assessment identified the importance of intensive treatment at an early a stage as possible, it also raised a question about his dangerousness. This presented something of a dilemma for the probation officer in preparing the PSR. This difficulty is highlighted in Hawkes' extremely valuable article on PSR's and child sexual abusers (1992):

> *The officer recognises that honest disclosure of (this) information is an encouraging sign and taken together with other factors may be persuaded to argue for a probation order. However the presentation of such alarming material is likely to raise the court's anxiety and achieve the opposite effect.*

Whilst observing that there are no easy answers to such problems, Hawkes proposes that such dilemmas may be mitigated by the way that written material is presented, by the PO's attendance at court to explain recommendations, and by shared training with sentencers. The HM Inspectorate Report (op.cit. 1991) identified effective reports in this area as those where:

> *If a recommendation was made for probation there was a description of the plan for supervision including methods to be used, the issues to be addressed and the sanctions which would be enacted.*

Although much of this will be familiar to most probation officers, in terms of good practice regarding PSR writing, it is particularly important in helping to emphasise parts of this process that are crucial to this area of work.

It is essential for the PO doing the report on Simon to gain sight of as much information as possible, including transcripts of the interviews with Simon and his victims. Additionally, it is important to gain knowledge from consultants, colleagues, and specialist agencies at as early a point in the process as possible.

Many specialists in the field have argued for changes in usual PSR preparation practice, whilst recognising the constraints on time and resources. The Greater Manchester Probation Service's Paper on *Work with Sex Offenders* (1994), for example, recommends that a minimum of two interviews need to be undertaken at the PSR stage (including when in custody) in order to assess the perpetrator's motivation to change their behaviour. Co-work is stressed as being particularly valuable at the pre-sentence stage in identifying an initial assessment of risk, and establishing a mode of work including inter-agency involvement.

Hawke emphasises the importance of gaining an understanding of those around the abuser (particularly, of course, where abuse has occurred within a family setting) as having a significant influence on the outcome of treatment. Such information may be gathered from other agencies involved, as well as through direct contact.

We have emphasised the importance of a thorough initial assessment by using the example of a PSR. However it is vital to re-emphasise that assessment is a continual process, particularly with such a high risk group where protection of the public is so crucial. Thus, at each stage of contact, change of contact, indeed every time they are seen, the progress and potential risk of re-offending should be considered, discussed with the relevant supervisor or other colleagues, recorded, and the appropriate action taken when and where necessary.

Methods of intervention

What is effective in this area of work is, of course, not necessarily dependent upon whether individual or group work is chosen, as the type of intervention. Good practice requires skills in the following areas:

- Assessment of risk as a necessary component throughout the course of contact (as discussed above).
- Clarity of aims and goals.

103

- Being able to work with an awareness of the feelings that such offending evokes.

- Holding purposefully to the goals set to reduce or control offending.

Not surprisingly, due to the pressures involved in managing such high risk work, group work approaches are seen to offer some of the most effective treatment options. Such approaches have the advantage of sharing the responsibilities, practice issues, dilemmas etc. for the worker. In addition, there is greater potential for more realistic discussion of offending in a group of offenders who are able to challenge patterns of denial and avoidance, as they themselves operate in this way. The membership of such groups will generally include men, who together have committed a wide range of different sexual offences, varying in seriousness, as it is usually felt that thinking and behaviour patterns are similar enough to be effectively treated or managed together.

Whilst individual work is often extremely effective, many workers will look to to the available group facilities, perhaps in addition to individual contact, as the most suitable type of intervention, both inside and outside prison.

Many probation areas have either developed particular sex offender programmes of their own or in partnership with other statutory or voluntary agencies. Cognitive behavioural techniques represent the most commonly used methods (in some format). Attempts to challenge the distorted thinking of offenders is seen as particularly appropriate in relation to aspects of denial, viewed as such a central concept in this type of work. A typical sex offender programme of this type is likely to include some or all of the following (Garrison 1992):

- obtaining a sexual history of each client,

- assessment,

- examination in depth of at least one significant offence,

- disclosure work,

- victims,

- attitudes to gender (power relationships, views about men and women),

- sexuality and children (for example, challenging misconceptions about children's sexuality),

- relationships,

- contributory factors (the impact of personal experiences and disinhibitors such as drugs and alcohol),

■ assertiveness,

■ power and control,

■ relapse prevention (learning techniques to prevent re-offending).

In addition, most programmes would probably explore each individual's specific pattern of offending, looking at it in terms of a cycle, where one incident or emotional response leads to another. This enables client and worker to identify triggers or danger signals, as well as points at which different choices might be made. The example below illustrates Simon's offending cycle:

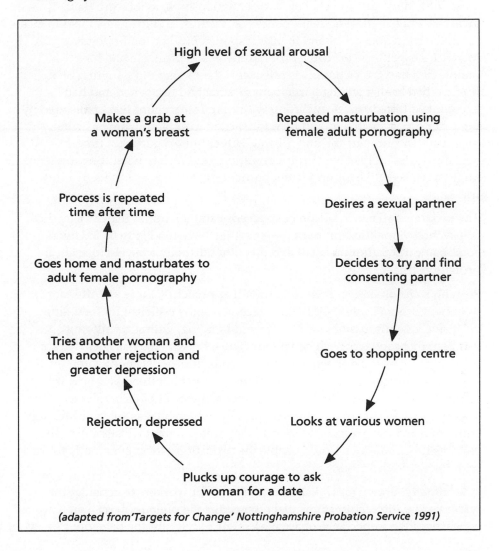

High level of sexual arousal

Makes a grab at a woman's breast

Repeated masturbation using female adult pornography

Process is repeated time after time

Desires a sexual partner

Goes home and masturbates to adult female pornography

Decides to try and find consenting partner

Tries another woman and then another rejection and greater depression

Goes to shopping centre

Rejection, depressed

Looks at various women

Plucks up courage to ask woman for a date

(adapted from'Targets for Change' Nottinghamshire Probation Service 1991)

It is clear from this cycle that there are several stages at which Simon could be encouraged to consider different choices. For example, at the point at which he recognises he feels depressed, he and the worker will need to identify an alternative course of action or type of behaviour which will alleviate these feelings without leading to the completion of the cycle.

Since 1992 the prison service has been introducing groupwork programmes for sex offenders, largely based upon a cognitive-behavioural approach. Those initially targetted had received sentences of four years or more. However, the inclusion of those serving shorter sentences, but who have been assessed as particularly dangerous, is planned. These programmes attempt to tackle offenders' distorted beliefs about relationships, to increase their awareness of the effect of their offences on victims, and to enable them to face up to the consequences of and to take responsibility for their offending. Maurice's experience of such a programme was typical. He had long maintained that the victim of his offences – the 12 year old daughter of a friend – had been a willing participant in what had happened and had encouraged his advances by flirting with him. His account was challenged by the other group members, and he was assisted to explore what he actually meant by 'encouragement' and 'flirting'. Over quite a period of time, he began to question his own perceptions and to appreciate what the experience might have been like for his victim, particularly as he was a trusted family friend.

The programmes run in prison have an educational, rather than any medical or psychotherapeutic, approach. To date they have tended to be led by a combination of uniformed staff and one other, usually a psychologist or a probation officer.

As with some other cognitive behavioural approaches, these sex offender treatment programmes (SOTP) have received some criticism for focussing exclusively on discussions of the current offending, without exploring complex root causes of such behaviour. Thus, Brown (1994) argues that for the programmes to be effective they have to include a psychodynamic exploration of the offenders' own victimisation in childhood and how it affected their adult lives. In Maurice's case, this would have involved a sensitive exploration of the physical abuse to which he was subjected during childhood and his position between his separated parents. Listening to the child victim in Maurice would enable the probation officer eventually to work with the adult victimiser.

Additionally, Brown (op.cit.) stresses the need for workers to consider the wider personality, motivations and interests of the offender with a view to considering the importance of a replacement activity for the behaviour given up. Thus behavioural techniques may have been of value, but they need to include other considerations and perspectives. Her comments apply equally to individual approaches and have parallels with similar considerations in the field of addictions.

Many of the exercises developed as part of groupwork programmes are translatable to individual approaches, such as those challenging patterns of thinking and behaviour. (See, for example, Nottinghamshire Probation Service pack 'Target's For Change' 1991). In the case of intra-familial offenders, services may favour a different approach which entails well planned and formulated inter-agency work. A pre-requisite for this is often that the offender takes responsibility for his actions.

In relation to individual work there is a decision that needs to be made between one to one or co-working (two workers to one client). Clearly there are many disadvantages of one to one work. Collusion, feelings of being overwhelmed by the type of information, or by the weight of responsibility, keeping focus in the face of continuing denial, overreaction and fear of the client. All of these are uncomfortable features, even with very good supervision, and many would feel that such involvement is unsuitable for inexperienced workers. Co-working helps to mitigate many of these difficulties and is often seen as more purposeful and effective as a result, although it is hard work, time intensive, and needs a lot of forethought and preplanning to work effectively. (See Paulson 1976 as quoted in Mark 1993). Critics of this approach point to the fact that such offenders tend to feel persecuted anyway and using two workers risks exacerbating such feelings.

Tackling denial

This is one of the overriding aspects of work with sex offenders. They are likely to deny the extent of their offending – "I don't know what came over me – I've never done anything like this before" – they are likely to deny the full effects on the victim – "It was just a bit of fun – she's probably forgotten all about it by now" – and they are likely to deny responsibility for what happened – "She led me on and I thought she enjoyed it".

There has been a lot of debate about the ethics of confrontational approaches in relation to work with sex offenders, with regard to groupwork in particular, but also in respect of individual approaches. Whilst some critics have viewed the more extreme examples as, 'legitimised nonce bashing' (Sheath 1990), most would recognise the need to challenge denial in this area of work. Both Mark (1993) and Hawkes (1992) make constructive and purposeful contributions to the debate by pointing out that denial is a process (rather than a door to be kicked down) which serves a particular function for sex offenders and needs to be approached with firmness of purpose, clarity and subtlety:

> *Although it is important to challenge dishonesty and distortion there are disadvantages in allowing the process of interviewing to degenerate into one of polarised accusation and denial. In such a situation we have noted that abusers are able to generate such a sense of self-pity at being (as they see it), unfairly harangued, that they are able to disassociate from the adult, scheming, sexually motivated side of their nature and retreat into the role of a vulnerable victim. A more productive approach is to make use of open ended, circular questions of the kind often employed in family therapy systems. (Hawkes 1992)*

Issues of denial are central in this area of work as they appear to make the aim of assessing risk so problematic. What is the balance between believing and not believing sex offending clients?

As contact with a high risk sex offender will often commence via throughcare (or an initial assessment at the PSR stage) establishing both purposeful contact and a realistic assessment can prove particularly difficult. Here the officer has to work hard to establish an effective working relationship, gain knowledge of the offender's progress in prison, and to relate their assessment to the particular circumstances (and risk of re-offending) on eventual release on licence. Such information will form the basis of the parole report and detail of the sentence plan.

Maurice's probation officer gained the impression that he had initially been reluctant to attend the sex offenders group in prison but had changed his mind at the last minute. The PO found it difficult to make sense of Maurice's attitude to his offending or the group. It seemed to switch from some acceptance of his sexual problems and difficulties to outright denial that he had been actually guilty of the particular offences for which he had received the prison sentence. As Maurice had experienced a number of changes of probation officer, this added to the difficulty of establishing a consistent process of assessment, particularly when visits were so infrequent, and detailed information about Maurice's progress – or lack of it – in prison was not easy to obtain.

The gaining of such information about offenders in the prison environment is, however, essential to a realistic assessment of risk that should form the basis of the planned work during the licence period. It is important to gain a clear idea of the extent to which Maurice is beginning to accept responsibility for his actions. If there is continued concern from the PO that such an assessment is not forthcoming, consideration may be given to try to establish such an assessment from specialised resources in the community (i.e. specialist sex offender workers, or teams where they exist, other forensic services, etc.). This will also help to establish suitable community treatment, where appropriate, and where this has not already been explored or established. So the probation officer working with Maurice at this stage is trying to make sense of his offence and the context within which it was originally committed, and to assess how things might be when he is released. What does his attitude to the offence reveal now? How has he responded to any treatment offered in prison? What might be the effect of the environment to which he is to return? What may trigger a return to such offending? What activities might replace it? These questions start to address the the vital issues of risk assessment from pre to post release. The importance of what Brown (1994) calls 'the continuity of oversight'.

Prior to Maurice's release the probation officer had also to consider monitoring his progress in relation to his future potential risk to the public. This would mean keeping a careful eye on the kind of employment he may gain recognising that certain types of work situation can pose a considerable risk and/or be exploited by some sex offenders. The balance between working with the client to reduce the risk of offending and protecting the public is particularly acute with this client group.

As Maurice was a 'schedule 1 offender' (someone having been convicted of an offence against a child or young person under the age of 18 under schedule 1 of the Children and Young Persons Act 1933), his PO had to ensure that procedures were followed in relation to checking and monitoring whether he intended to live either with a family or in a place where he had substantial access to children. The whereabouts and concerns of the victim and her family must also be thought about. The PO should consider whether any conditions should be attached to Maurice's licence prohibiting him from contacting the victim and her family. In cases where the probation officer makes a recommendation concerning a condition relating to the protection of children, there is a presumption that this will be accepted. (HM Prison Service Guidance Notes to Governors 54/1994):

> Prison probation staff have to notify the social services department in the area to which a schedule 1 offender is released.

Working with sex offenders represents one of the most difficult areas of probation practice, often evoking feelings of disbelief, horror, anger and disgust. In view of the difficulties inherent in making effective assessments and sustained interventions that reduce further offending and help to protect the future victims, many probation areas have moved towards specialisation. Thus PSRs are often now undertaken by officers with specialist knowledge and training, and co-working and consultancy are seen to be an increasingly necessary adjunct to assessment at the pre-sentence stage. The number of groupwork and multi-agency schemes has increased, often providing pre-release assessment, particularly in relation to establishing release on parole as a condition of a group treatment programme.

These moves towards shared assessment and practice are a testament to both the importance and high risk nature of this type of work. For those wishing to move into specialising in this type of work, intensive support supervision and training are essential as the newer officer becomes more familiar with dilemmas, administrative procedures and emotional wear and tear. There are sound arguments for not insisting that those who feel completely antipathetic to this type of work be forced to undertake it, as this may result in particularly poor practice. It should not be forgotten that probation officers themselves may have been the victims of sexual abuse.

What is clear is that no worker should ever feel tempted under pressure to go it alone. Consultation and support are essential at every stage.

REFERENCES

1. Abel, G., Becker, J., Cunningham-Rathner, J. and Rouleau, J. (1987) 'Self Reported Sex Crimes of 561 Nonincarcerated Paraphiliacs', in *Journal of Interpersonal Violence*, 2, 60, pp. 3-25

2. Brown, A (1994) *Suggested Reforms To The Sex Offender Treatment Programme*, Prison Reform Trust.

3. See Dalrymple, J. (1993) 'Judges in the Dock', in *The Sunday Times News Review*, 13 June, Times Publishers

4. Dominelli, L (1991) *Gender, Sex Offenders & Probation Practice*, Novata Press

5. Elliott, M. (ed.) (1993) *Female Sexual Abuse of Children: The Last Taboo*, Longman

6. Finkelhor, D. and Russell,D. (1984) *Women as Perpetrators* in Finkelhor, D. (ed.) *Child Sexual Abuse: New Theory and Research*, New York: Free Press

7. Finkelhor, D.(1987) in Horobin, G, (ed.) *Sex, Gender and Care Work*, London: Jessica Kingsley

8. Garrison, K (1992) *Working with Sex Offenders*, UEA Monograph

9. Gilyeat, D. (1994) *A Companion Guide to Offence Seriousness*, Owen Wells Publishers

10. Gocke, B. (1991) *Tackling Denial in Sex Offenders*, UEA Monograph

11. Greater Manchester Probation Service (1994) *Managment Of Work With Sex Offenders*, (Paper 2)

12. Hawkes, C. (1992) 'An Integrated Approach To The Preparation Of Social Enquiry Reports Concerning Child Sexual Abusers', in *Beyond Containment The Penal Response to Sex Offending*, Prison Reform Trust

13. HM Inspectorate Of Probation (1991) *The Work Of the Probation Service with Sex Offenders*, Home Office

14. HM Prison Service (1994) *Guidance Notes to Governors, 54/1994*, Home Office

15. Hurley, W. and Monahan, T. M. (1969) 'Arson: The Criminal and The Crime', in *British Journal of Criminology*, Vol.9, pp. 4-21

16. Jennings, K. T. (1993) 'Female Child Molestation: A Review of the Literature', in Elliott, M. (ed.) *Female Sexual Abuse of Children: The Last Taboo*, Longman

17. Mark. P. 'Training Staff to Work with Sex Offenders', in *NAPO Journal*, March 1992

18. McColl, A. and Hargreaves. R. 'Explaining Sex Offending, in Court Reports', in *NAPO Journal*, March 1993

19. Moore, J. 'Confronting the Perpetrators', in *Community Care*, 12 April 1990

20. Morrison, T., Eroga, M. and Beckett, R. C. (eds.) (1994) *Sexual Offending Against Children: Assessment and Treatment of Male Abusers*, Routledge

21. Nottinghamshire Probation Service (1991) *Targets for Change*, Nottinghamshire Probation Service

22. O'Callaghan, D, and Print, B. (1994) 'Adolescent Sexual Abusers; Research, Assessment and Treatment' in Morrison, T. (ed.) *Sexual Offending Against Children*, Routledge

23. Richardson, G. 'Juvenile Sexual Perpetrators: A Model Approach & The Role of the Probation Service', in *Probation Journal*, December 1990

24. Prins, H. (1986) *Dangerous Behaviour, The Law & Mental Disorder*, Tavistock

25. Sampson, A. (1994) *Acts of Abuse: Sex Offenders and the Criminal Justice System*, Routledge

26. Saunders, A. and Senior, P. (1994) *Jarvis' Probation Officers' Manual*, 5th Edition Sheffield Hallam

27. Scully, D. (1990) *Understanding Sexual Violence*, Harper Collins

28. Sheath, M. (1990) 'Confrontative Work with Sex Offenders: Legitimised Nonce Bashing' in *Probation Journal*, 37:4 pp. 159-62

29. Smith, H, and Israel, E. (1987) 'Sibling Incest: A Study of the Dynamics of 25 Cases', in *Child Abuse and Neglect*, 2

30. Waterhouse, L., Dobash, R. and Carnie, J. (1994) *Child Sexual Abusers*, Scottish Office

31. Wyre. R (1987) *Women, Men & Rape*, Oxford Perry Publishers

7
Working with mental health problems

Many of the clients of the probation service suffer from some kind of mental health problem – from depression, neuroses of one kind or another, alcohol/ drug abuse, to more serious kinds of mental illness – mania, schizophrenia or psychotic disorders. Our clients can also be suffering from mental disorder/ confusion associated with their developmental stage; for instance, an adolescent might become quite depressed or withdrawn, being unable to cope with the conflict and turmoil which growing into adulthood might present. The so called mid-life crisis may involve quite acute depression to do with not having fulfilled one's hopes and aspirations. There are also people suffering from what is termed a 'personality disorder' for whom treatment is often not considered to be an option, but who form a particularly vulnerable group in society.

People with mental health problems present a range of difficulties for social work professionals. They can often pose a risk both to themselves and to others, their life styles are often unsettled and they can be used and abused by others. Resources in the community for those with mental health problems are limited and often patchy depending on where you live; resources that also cater for the range of cultural differences are limited too. People who suffer from mental illness often end up in the prison system quite inappropriately because there is nowhere else safe to put them. You have to be deemed very ill to warrant hospital treatment and, as a consequence, many people who are not OK but are not considered treatable, end up on probation when they offend.

The number of probation service clients with some degree of mental health problem has been gradually increasing and will probably continue to do so. The mental strain caused by poverty, homelessness, prolonged unemployment, and persecution and oppression remains a pervading fact of our society and the response to this constellation of pressures can often be to offend. The aftermath of community care and the changes in the social security system has resulted in more confused and lost people on the streets, who may resort to illegal means in order to survive.

A further increase in this particular client group stems from changes to post release arrangements under the Criminal Justice Act 1991. Everyone sentenced to more than 12 months imprisonment now comes out on licence and is under supervision (except fine defaulters, contempt of courters and deportees!) of whom some will have had mental health problems. Research suggests that approximately 17 per cent of males, 19.9 per cent of young adults, and 57 per cent of women in prison have been diagnosed as suffering from some degree of mental disorder and potentially this has enormous implications (Gunn Report 1991).

This is a client group that causes much concern among probation officers. How much do we need to know about types of mental illness and relevant symptoms? Although clearly not qualified to diagnose, we certainly need to be able to make an assessment about a client's level of 'alrightness'. How can this best be done? What are the processes that lead individuals with mental health problems into the criminal justice system and what resources and types of intervention are available? These are some of the questions that we are now going to try to answer. After all, you never know when mental health issues might arise....

You are on court duty one dull November day when Sandy appears charged with affray. She is in a very agitated state, seems unable to understand the questions the clerk to the court is putting to her, and you are asked by the magistrates to see if you can assist in some way. No duty psychiatrist was available at this particular court. What should you do?

A probation officer in the community supervision team is interviewing William, a new client, who is subject to a probation order and has just been transferred in from another area. Information to hand is scanty as the client's file and copy of his PSR has not arrived yet. The client has arrived on spec, asking for a grant to enable him to buy stuff for his new home. The client tells the PO he believes he is possessed by the spirit of his dead twin brother who is dictating poetry to him. The PO's heart sinks. He is recently qualified and realises he has left his Diploma in Social Work at home ... what should he do?

These are just two examples that illustrate the lively and varied life of the probation officer in general, and possible dilemmas posed by mental health problems in particular.

❏ What is mental illness?

This is a pertinent, if overambitious, question to attempt to answer as a backdrop to what follows. Clearly a simplistic view would suggest a state of 'not alrightness' which may have a number of causes. Within this a distinction can be made between on the one hand organic mental illness – with an identifiable physical cause – and on the other what Szasz (1977) suggests are 'problems of living' and what Laing (1964) argues is a sensible response to the unbearable pressures of the a system in which we find ourselves, whether familial or social.

Individuals may retreat into an unusual state for a range of reasons; in considering these states, we must however bear in mind all the differences which distinguish us from one another. Our responses to stress or crisis might be inexplicable in one culture and perfectly understandable in another (Rack 1982). This clearly has implications for interpretation, professional response and for treatment. It is a well documented fact that in Britain black people are four times more likely to be admitted under compulsory sections of the Mental Health Act 1983, and 12 times more likely to receive a diagnosis of schizophrenia. Of those who come before the courts, black mentally disordered offenders are more likely than similar white offenders to be subject to the police and criminal sections of the Mental Health Act rather than the civil sections. Also they are more likely to be detained in conditions of high security (Royal College of Psychiatrists 1990; NACRO 1990;1991).

The reasons for such differential treatment are complex, involving a number of interrelating factors – institutional racism within the health and criminal justice systems, myths and stereotypes concerning dangerousness, the previous experiences of black people in their contact with the authorities and a failure to offer appropriate assistance to some black people at the onset of their illness. In addition, people from other cultures who deal with life's exigencies in ways which do not conform to white, western norms are more likely to be labelled mad than the indigenous population. By the same token, women are also discriminated against in this regard, since frequently the criminal justice system prefers to explain their offending as 'mad' rather than 'bad' in order to account for some of the 'unwomanly' things that they do (Worrall 1990).

It has been estimated that a higher proportion of women than men suffer from mental disorder at some point in their lives and the rate of admission to psychiatric hospital is also higher. When we translate this to the criminal justice system we find that although the number of women offenders compared with men is very low, a larger proportion of women offenders appear to suffer from a mental disorder. Gunn's research, published in 1992, found that 56 per cent of female prisoners had mental health problems and a Home Office Report in 1993 entitled *A Profile of Mentally Disordered Offenders in The Approved Probation and Bail Hostel System* found that 23.57 per cent of female residents had received psychiatric treatment in the previous 12 months, as opposed to only 11.7 per cent of male residents. Despite this, facilities tend to be dominated by the needs of men and not women, as offending is a predominantly male activity.

Mental illness is, of course, a complex area – some clients are cheerfully eccentric and this has positives and strengths; some people retreat into an unusual state to deal with the dreadful reality of their existence – who can blame them? This is fine as long as they can remain safe, stay clear of trouble, and find a way of managing that does not bring them into conflict with the law. But what if they don't? How do you respect people's idiosyncrasies on the one hand, but protect them (and others) on the other? This is all about tightropes and how to walk them. It is here of course that our approach to difference becomes crucial; equally crucial are the powerful processes that come into play in relation to psychiatric services, the mechanics of labelling and the ensuing stereotypes that can haunt individuals long after the crisis has passed.

❑ Types of mental disorders

There is no universal acceptance of any one classification of mental disorders although the World Health Organisation has a go at this from time to time. Here we are relying on the outline classification offered by Prins (1980, p. 54):

- the functional psychoses (affective disorders, schizophrenia);
- the neuroses (mild depression, anxiety states, hysteria, obsessional states);
- personality disorders including psychopathy, abnormalities of personality and psycho-sexual disorders;
- alcohol and other drug addictions;
- mental disorder as a result of infection, disease, metabolic disturbance and trauma (for example epilepsy);
- mental disorder due to the ageing process (a condition such as Alzheimer's disease);

- mental abnormalities (deficiency, handicap, learning difficulties including chromosomal abnormalities).

Within the scope of this chapter it will be impossible to deal with all these areas in detail. Issues related to drugs and alcohol and the question of how helpful a medical model or psychiatric model is to these client groups have been dealt with elsewhere. We have chosen, therefore, to focus on the first three categories, as probation officers are more likely to be working with people who have had these labels attached to them.

The functional psychoses

This term is used for the group of severe mental disorders in which no evidence of underlying organic brain dysfunction has yet been proved to exist.

Two main illnesses in this category are:

- Depressive and manic depressive illness.
- Schizophrenic illness.

Depressive and manic depressive illness (affective disorders)

These include severe depressive disorder or psychotic depression, manic – depressive disorders and hypermania. They are characterised by disturbance of mood or affect, ranging from mild, where the mood change may be only slight and often hard to spot, to severe forms.

In the latter, the main characteristics are those of 'loss' – of energy, libido, weight, appetite, interest in self – and abject misery and tearfulness. This condition used to be called 'melancholia' for obvious reasons. In addition there may be restlessness, lack of concentration, sleep disturbance, preoccupation with bodily functions (e.g. that insides are rotting away) and suicidal thoughts and actions.

The illness may be punctuated by manic episodes and, in this form, is referred to as manic depression. Behaviour may include hyperactivity, excitability, loss of inhibitions, and grandiose ideas. People can become violent if restrained or checked. Hypomania is a related illness though not as extreme.

These conditions may be triggered by a particular event or crisis – a bereavement for instance – but this is not necessarily the case. Sometimes a person simply becomes ill with no apparent precipitating factor. The former is often referred to as 'reactive' (depression) and the latter as 'endogenous' (depression).

Schizophrenic illnesses

Controversy still rages about the origins of schizophrenia. Is it nature or nurture? What is the relative significance of environmental, biological and genetic factors? No one really knows what causes schizophrenia, if the truth be told. Different kinds have been identified, including simple schizophrenia, paranoid schizophrenia and catatonic schizophrenia.

The common image of the schizophrenic as a 'split personality', a Jekyll and Hyde character, is something of a myth. In fact what schizophrenics suffer from is a terrifying splintering of the mind, where thoughts become disordered into lots of disconnected fragments and the individual's personality begins to disintegrate. It is not surprising that family and friends often say something to the effect of "He's unrecognisable as the person I used to know."

People suffering from this illness may experience delusions, for instance believing they are famous people or CIA agents. They may suffer from hallucinations, hearing voices that tell them what to do or seeing things or people that aren't there. The belief that thoughts can be heard or controlled by others – receiving messages through the radio or television – is not uncommon and this can often lead to unprovoked attacks.

At times people can appear apathetic and withdrawn; they may have periods where they are motionless, seeming in a trance-like state and this is referred to as catatonia. It may be followed by unpredictable violence.

The neuroses

These usually originate in some kind of mental conflict of which the sufferer may frequently be unaware. Neuroses are less dangerous than psychoses, because the sufferer usually stays in touch with reality, the symptoms are less florid, and the person behaves more or less normally most of the time. However, neurotic conditions can be severely disabling, despite the fact that many of us use the term 'neurotic' jokingly and often to describe ourselves or our nearest and dearest! The neuroses should not be regarded as diseases but as ways of reacting to stress. They are sometimes referred to as illnesses because the response is maladaptive – that is, it does not help to resolve the stress and indeed may make it worse.

Symptoms include mild depression, where the sufferer may suddenly depart from usual and expected modes of behaviour – for example, they may begin to shop-lift. They can experience extreme anxiety which may be about something in particular or non specific – anxiety about everything at once, a free floating, nameless dread, causing palpitations, nausea, giddiness, loss of appetite, or feelings of suffocation.

Phobias and obsessive states are also classified as neuroses. These are characterised by the compulsive need to carry out certain actions or go through certain thought processes or avoid certain things. We all have a tendency to be obsessive or phobic about something (socks on the dressing table; spiders etc.). The significant shift is when such a phobia or obsession starts to interfere with normal life.

Personality disorders

The term 'personality disorder' abounds in the criminal justice system, and is often attached to a person whose behaviour is very obviously, decidedly odd and anti-social, but cannot be explained with reference to any of the other categories of mental illness. One might suspect it is a dustbin term – a place to put all the people whose illnesses you don't understand.

The General Registrar's Office in its *Glossary of Mental Disorders*, to which you might be tempted to spring for assistance, is not in fact terribly helpful. This is what it says:

> *This category refers to a group of more or less well defined anomalies or deviations of personality which are not the result of psychosis or any other illness. The differentiation of these personalities is to some extent arbitrary and the reference to a given group will depend initially on the relative predominance of one or other group of character traits....*
> *(General Register Office 1968, Glossary of Mental Disorders, Prins 1980, p. 86)*

See what we mean! PRM put in for a few days leave after grappling with this one.

Psychopathy

This is a type of personality disorder, and although the two terms are often used interchangeably, this is very misleading. Whereas someone with a personality disorder can be difficult, anti-social and very definitely not alright, a psychopathic personality is distinguished by additional disturbing and troubling characteristics.

These include a complete lack of concern for the feelings or welfare of others, and an absence of guilt, shame or remorse about the effect of their actions.

People suffering from this condition tend to be entirely focussed on themselves, and are incapable of showing affection and love towards others. They are insincere, are not averse to telling lies, and are frequently very plausible and even charming, with no obvious signs of mental illness.

❑ Mental health and legal responsibility

As we have seen from the story so far, the term 'mental illness' broadly means a state of mind which affects mood, judgment and behaviour. The term you will also see quite a bit in the legislation and guidelines is 'mentally disordered' – a legal term pertaining to the Mental Health Act 1983 which distinguishes four categories:

- **Mental disorder** – mental illness, incomplete development of mind, any disorder or disability of mind.

- **Severe mental impairment** – incomplete development of mind, impairment of intelligence and social functioning, associated with seriously aggressive or irresponsible conduct.

- **Mental impairment** – a lesser form of the above.

- **Psychopathic disorder** – a disability of mind, not necessarily due to impairment of intelligence, which results in abnormally aggressive or irresponsible conduct.

As you can see, these categories are in some ways artificial and don't take us much further forward – it's the terminology which is relevant here.

❑ Mental health and the criminal justice system

After years of invisibility, poor service and discrimination, the needs of offenders with mental health problems have recently become the focus of considerable attention following the publication of Home Office Circular 66/ 90 *Provision for Mentally Disordered Offenders* and the Reed Report 1991 *The Review of Health and Social Services for Mentally Disordered Offenders and Others Requiring Similar Services*. Both these documents have drawn a attention to the importance of diverting the mentally disordered offender from the criminal justice system to the health service and ensuring that statutory and voluntary agencies work together to provide appropriate support and services. Although this is the ideal to which all energies should be directed, it is very early days. Many schemes are in very embryonic form and the recent tragic cases that have hit the headlines suggest that there is still a long way to go, as with all aspects of community care.

This is highlighted by *The Report of the Enquiry into the Care and Treatment of Christopher Clunis* (1994) which presents a sad catalogue of poor communication, dubious judgments, mistakes and inadequate facilities involving a variety of different agencies.

The probation officer's role in relation to people with mental health problems and the criminal justice process raises two questions:

■ Which are the relevant bits of the 1983 Mental Health Act in relation to probation practice?

■ What are the courts' options and how does the probation officer's role fit in?

The first point of contact between the criminal justice system and the disordered person is often the police, who may be called to intervene in cases where someone is behaving in an unusual or unacceptable way in a public place – talking loudly to themselves, appearing distressed, behaving inappropriately towards others.

Section 136 of the 1983 Mental Health Act allows the police to remove such a person from a public place to a place of safety for their own protection and that of others. They may be detained for up to 72 hours and arrangements are then made for the person to be assessed by a psychiatrist and seen by a social worker approved under the mental health act (known as an ASW) within that time. Detention should ideally be in a hospital not a police station.

What actually happens of course depends on various factors, and here the crucial aspects of race and gender play a part – as they do at all points in the criminal justice process. What is seen by some as acceptable behaviour in men is often not in women – urinating in the high street for example. We are all aware of the frequency with which people from non western cultures get labelled as mentally disordered because their behaviour is misunderstood, and their reactions to situations may be different. Police responses to unusual behaviour also differ. In some instances the police are called but take no action; in other cases a sensitive, multi-disciplinary approach operates, and in others there is a level of crass brutality and ignorance.

In the case of minor offences the police have the option to caution. If the behaviour is sufficiently serious to warrant a charge being brought, the next stage in the process is for details to be sent to the Crown Prosecution Service (CPS) who will determine whether it is in the public interest to proceed. At this point people with mental health difficulties who have committed minor offences, or who are first offenders, should be diverted from the court system.

If people are going to be diverted from the criminal justice system, however, it is vital that they are linked in with the appropriate health and social services to meet their needs and are not simply set adrift. The report of the Clunis Inquiry vividly demonstrates that there are occasions when diversion from the courts is neither in the best interests of the individual nor public safety. The report underlines just how important it is that:

> A medical opinion from a forensic medical examiner is always obtained by the police if it appears to them that an offender is suffering from mental illness and so that the potential seriousness of the offence and the public interest is always taken into account in deciding whether to charge. (Clunis Report 1994)

❑ The role of the probation officer in court

Let us now move on to look at what happens to those who are not diverted pre-court but do go on to appear. As Burney says:

> Magistrates courts especially in inner cities frequently find themselves acting as the agents of control for what are essentially social problems and in no sense is this more true than in the case of mentally disordered offenders. (1992)

It is of course at this point – the entry of the person into the court system – that the probation service usually comes on the scene. Here you, as the court duty officer, can intervene in a number of ways.

Firstly, although probation officers are of course not qualified to make psychiatric diagnoses, they are in a position to make an informal assessment about a person's level of 'alrightness' and to bring this to the attention of the court. There may be a question about whether the person is actually fit to plead – that is, able to understand the charges, follow and understand the evidence and instruct a legal representative. This can only be assessed by a psychiatrist and the defendant would normally be declared unfit to plead only if they are severely mentally ill or impaired. Such a status can have grave consequences, such as being detained in a psychiatric hospital or in custody for an indefinite period.

An increasing number of courts, particularly in inner city areas, have a duty psychiatric service available to them on certain days of the week. When Sandy appeared in court there was, of course, no such service and so the bench asked the court duty probation officer to see her. Her first task was to calm

Sandy down and it became clear that she did know what was going on and she understood the charges although she was in a very distressed state. The court duty officer then tried to discover from Sandy whether she was known to any other local services and, if so, whether she was receiving any treatment. Sandy was not prepared to give much away at all but did mention that she was on probation in an adjoining area. So the court duty officer was able to phone her probation officer for further information. Meanwhile, Sandy was seen by the duty solicitor. When she went back in court and pleaded guilty, the court duty officer was then able to advise the bench that she had spoken to Sandy's probation officer and it seemed that a PSR and psychiatric report would be of assistance.

If the offence is considered to be a minor one, the court may take the view that the matter should be dealt with simply and speedily, irrespective of the apparent mental health difficulties of the defendant. The court duty officer should then take a proactive role by seeing the person afterwards in case any help is required or, if appropriate, to link them in with a local resource.

When a defendant with mental health problems is to be remanded by the court, then every effort should be made to divert them from custody. The court duty officer will be involved in gathering as much information as possible about their situation and support systems within the community, or exploring the possibilities of a hostel placement. Vulnerable clients may be at risk of being remanded in custody simply because their way of life is perceived by the court as unstable, and they may be regarded as better off or safer behind bars, particularly if substance abuse is a factor – prison can be seen as a useful means of detoxification.

A recent Home Office study found that disproportionately large numbers of mentally disordered offenders are remanded in custody simply for the preparation of psychiatric reports, and often they have committed relatively minor offences. The report referred to the practice as "inhumane, expensive and ineffective" (Mentally Disordered Remand Prisoners, Home Office 1991). If a remand on bail is not practical, a court can, on the advice of an approved medical practitioner, remand a mentally disordered offender to hospital for the preparation of a psychiatric report (Section 35, Mental Health Act 1983).

❑ The PSR stage

Preparing a report on somebody with mental health difficulties, who may or may not be potentially dangerous, can be a complex, time consuming and stressful task. The interviews themselves may be difficult to conduct and will require all the skill, sensitivity and patience that one can muster. It is vital to take what is said seriously and to struggle to separate fact from fantasy, rather than assuming that everything is a product of the individual's mental state. Once it is apparent that someone has mental health problems, there may be an issue about the number of interviews required to gather all the information, and it will probably be necessary to contact quite a number of other professionals both for information about the defendant's history and to explore options for treatment and support.

Assessing the extent to which the offending behaviour is associated with the mental health problems can be a difficult process, but it is essential in order to make any constructive suggestions to the court in terms of what is required to reduce the risk of further offending, as well as to protect the public.

In William's case, for instance, there was clearly a link. He made an unprovoked attack on a fellow passenger on the bus, believing she was intercepting messages from his dead brother. He has been diagnosed as a paranoid schizophrenic and if this were to remain untreated, then the likelihood of re-offending and further risk to the public may be considerable.

It is essential that anybody preparing a PSR on a mentally disordered offender liaises thoroughly with all other professionals involved, particularly with the psychiatrist, if one is preparing a report. This will ensure that the court is eventually presented with a proposal which is workable, agreed and authoritative.

❏ Sentencing options

Despite the cases that hit the headlines it's important to remember that the vast majority of mentally disordered offenders commit relatively minor offences which are unlikely to warrant a custodial sentence (Hodgkins 1993).

Fines and discharges

Had William merely threatened somebody on the bus rather than physically attacking them, the writer of the PSR might well have argued that the offence was not sufficiently serious to warrant a community sentence. However, William would still clearly have had needs in relation to his illness and it would have been important for the probation officer to put him in touch with the appropriate services for treatment and support. All this would need to be spelled out in the conclusion of the report. If not, the court would very likely think in terms of a probation order in the hope of meeting

William's needs rather than because it would be warranted by the seriousness of his offence.

Community penalties

It is unlikely that anyone with a serious mental health problem would be able to comply with the strenuous demands of a community service or combination order, even if the restriction of liberty criterion is met. The question of suitability must always be addressed and in the case of a combination order whether "the offender has a reasonable prospect of completing the order successfully" (National Standards 1992; 1995).

In addition to the ordinary probation order without conditions, the court has the power to make a probation order with a condition of psychiatric treatment (either in or outpatient treatment) or a probation order with a condition of residence. Both these orders, of course, involve a considerable restriction of an individual's liberty and should be reserved for serious offenders.

In the case of a mentally disordered offender, a condition of residence may be to a specialist hostel such as the Richmond Fellowship (check current name) or to a therapeutic community such as the Henderson Hospital. There is, however, a desperate shortage of residential provision and assessment procedures may be complex and lengthy, involving not only assessment by the individual establishment but also by the local authority for community care funding. Because provision is limited, it can sometimes be tempting to use establishments which will accept all comers, without rigorous assessment procedures. Needless to say, this is to be avoided as it could make matters much worse.

The number of probation orders made with a condition of psychiatric treatment has been diminishing over the years, from 1,530 in 1982 to 903 in 1991 (Probation Statistics 1991, Home Office). The court must receive written or oral evidence from an approved medical practitioner that the defendant would benefit from psychiatric treatment and that it is available, but that the condition is not so serious as to warrant detention under a hospital order.

The declining use of these orders, when there is clearly no corresponding decline in the numbers of mentally disordered offenders appearing before the courts, may have something to do with their somewhat paradoxical nature. Since the probation order became a sentence in its own right, with the Criminal Justice Act 1991, extra conditions are concerned primarily with restriction of liberty rather than the needs of the offender, and this does not fit easily with the concepts of voluntarism, patient choice and confidentiality

125

which have traditionally prevailed within the health service. There are many who continue to hold the view that there is no point in attempting treatment unless a client/patient is motivated, and if they are motivated, then the condition of treatment is redundant.

In their inspection of probation orders with requirements of psychiatric treatment The Home Office Inspectorate found:

> *Many of the offenders in the sample presented the courts with agonising decisions, balancing culpability,sympathy for the offender, danger to the public, fear of violence and madness, bizarre behaviour and strong defence pleading. It seemed likely that quite often probation orders with requirements for treatment were seen as a way out of the court's dilemma, rather than a more objective decision based on soundly prepared and weighted expert evidence from doctor and probation officer alike. (Home Office 1993)*

The inspectors found that there was considerable variation between areas regarding provision and arrangements for the preparation of psychiatric reports and that facilities were patchy. This often seemed to them to depend upon historical factors or the personalities involved.

Hospital orders

Under **Section 37 of the Mental Health Act 1983,** the court may make a hospital order as an alternative to a penal disposal if it is satisfied, on the evidence of two medical practitioners, that the person is suffering from one of the four categories defined by the Act, and that a bed will be available within 28 days. There does not necessarily have to be a link between the defendant's mental state and the offence, and the person can be detained in hospital for up to six months, the authority to detain being renewable.

In the case of the most serious offenders, the Crown Court, having made a hospital order, can, under **Section 41 of the Mental Health Act 1983**, make a further order restricting the discharge or transfer of the person without the consent of the Home Secretary. The purpose of such a restriction order is to protect the public, and risk to the public must be proved. The Home Secretary has the power to discharge somebody unconditionally or with conditions. The conditions would usually include residence, supervision by a local psychiatrist and by a 'social supervisor'. The social supervisor may be a local authority social worker, but is frequently a probation officer.

Section 47 of the Mental health Act 1983 enables a person to be transferred from prison to hospital if the Home Secretary is satisfied by the reports of two registered medical practitioners that the prisoner is suffering from one of the four categories of mental disorder, the nature or degree of which warrants detention in a psychiatric hospital for treatment.

Those who pose a serious risk to the public and cannot be safely managed in a local psychiatric hospital, are likely to be admitted to either a regional secure unit which provides conditions of medium security, or to one of the special hospitals (Broadmoor, Rampton or Ashworth) which provide conditions of high security. It will come as no surprise to hear, however, that there is a chronic shortage of beds and so it is likely that mentally disordered offenders who really should not be in prison, will continue to be held for the foreseeable future in grossly unsuitable conditions where the only treatment available is drugs.

In May 1994, the Chief Inspector of Prisons, in his report on Wakefield Prison, was very critical of the lack of treatment within the NHS for offenders with severe mental health problems. He found about 50 housed on the ordinary wing in:

> What appeared to be a semi-sedated condition ... We were concerned that their safety was solely reliant on vigilant staff and the tolerance of other inmates. Efforts to get these inmates transferred to special hospitals were not succeeding. (Tumin 1994)

❏ Practice issues

We hope by now you've got the message that diversion from the criminal justice system to the health and social services is the order of the day in working with mentally disordered offenders. That is, diversion at any appropriate point in the process – at the point of arrest, pre-court, at the court stage, on conviction and from prison.

The probation officer on the ground could be forgiven for not realising this as there remains a large gap between policy and practice in some areas. However, if not diverted appropriately, many people with mental health problems will get caught up in the perpetual cycle of petty offending and imprisonment so familiar to workers in the criminal justice system and highlighted by NACRO's study *Revolving Doors* (1992). In reality, effective diversion depends to a large extent on strategic planning and co-operation between all the relevant agencies – health, social services, probation and the voluntary sector – working together is an essential prerequisite. Some areas have already gone a long way down this road and provide an impressive example to others, for instance, having set up multi-disciplinary forensic teams comprising psychiatrists, psychologists, community psychiatric nurses (CPNs), social workers and probation officers. These teams, sadly by no means the norm at the present time, are able to respond quickly at each stage in the process, to facilitate diversion at the outset, assessment in court, to provide a PSR and to provide appropriate treatment. It means a readily identifiable local focus for responsibility and expertise, effective communication and support, and an approach which is multi-disciplinary.

For those of us not fortunate enough to have access to a specialist forensic team, effective liaison and communication with the other professionals involved is, of course, equally important, particularly at significant points – at the report stage, immediately after sentence, and at the end of an order or at the point of breach. It is essential to share information and to be clear about the respective roles and objectives of each of the principal players – probation officer, CPN and psychiatrist.

In many ways, a clear psychiatric diagnosis, where the condition is seen to be amenable to treatment, is not only good news for the individual but for the probation officer as well. In the case of William, diagnosed as a paranoid schizophrenic, the psychiatrist sees him on a regular basis, and administers injections. In addition, a CPN visits him at home at regular intervals, so the probation officer is simply able to pick up the phone and share any anxieties about changes in his moods, behaviour or attitudes and vice versa. The three professionals involved have meetings every few months in order to review William's progress and their respective roles.

As we know, however, many of our clients do not have such a clear diagnosis as William. They are those people who tread the thin line between being not OK but not 'un-OK' enough to warrant medical help. Here we find ourselves returning to the group of people labelled 'personality disorders'. The Home Office Inspectors found that "some psychiatrists were willing to struggle in partnership with the probation service in the management and re-education of such offenders. Other psychiatrists considered them not a medical problem". In addition, "probation officers showed considerable perseverance in 'staying with' these very difficult offenders". This takes us to the crux of the matter since it is this very task of "staying with" that gives rise to a range of anxieties for the worker, especially if your client is not considered to be a medical problem, and you are in fact the only professional involved with them.

Sandy highlights many of the dilemmas posed by clients with a personality disorder. First, it is impossible to apply National Standards as she frequently refuses to leave the house or turns up at the office unexpectedly, drunk or under the influence of drugs, demanding to be seen immediately and threatening to create havoc if her demands are not met. In the thematic inspection of probation orders with requirements for psychiatric treatment "it became clear that National Standards did not entirely fit mentally disordered offenders". Frequent phone calls from Sandy's mother and the neighbours, who are all at the end of their tether, add to the burden of responsibility the worker carries – somebody has got to do something, or they are going to the papers. Sandy has no GP to whom the PO can turn, and is not prepared to seek any help herself. She has frequently demonstrated that she is a risk to others, and her previous overdoses prove that she is also a serious risk to herself.

Mentally disordered offenders are in fact more likely to be a danger to themselves than to others. Serious mental disorder and alcohol misuse greatly increase the chances of somebody committing suicide. There is no truth in the notion that people who talk about suicide will never actually kill themselves. When people tell you they have thought about or are thinking about suicide, they must be taken seriously. It should also be remembered that asking somebody whether they have had any suicidal thoughts is not going to make them more likely to kill themselves. On the contrary, approached in a sensitive and concerned way, addressing the possibility may actually reduce the risk, as the person is likely to feel better understood.

At times Sandy becomes depressed. People who are very depressed or anxious or who feel persecuted and as though they are disintegrating, are very painful to work with. Often we end up feeling some of their feelings; often we experience a sense of hopelessness. The urge to do something becomes very pressing because it makes us feel better. Often, though, what such clients need more than anything is for someone to take their pain seriously, acknowledge that it can't be taken away right now and just stay alongside, trying hard to put themselves in the client's shoes, even for a short while. Sometimes it is impossible to know how best to support or contain; on occasion the feelings are too pervasive and powerful. Providing a safe place for fears and fantasies, where some of one's more baffling thoughts can be shared, would not be a bad aim.

Working with people like Sandy can be very frustrating, to put it mildly. It will often seem that however many hours the worker puts in, however understanding and supportive the approach, nothing ever changes. There may be the odd glimmer of light on the horizon, when Sandy comes in, articulate, sober and lucid, asking you to make an appointment with the clinical psychologist or to refer her to a hostel because she knows she can't go on like this. You clutch this straw with a huge sense of relief – help is at hand for both of you – make umpteen phone calls, fill in a few lengthy forms, only then to be told in no uncertain terms that Sandy has changed her mind.

Working with mentally disordered offenders is frequently a process of taking one step forward and two steps back. Whilst it can be difficult, it is vital to hang on to the fact that 'staying with' somebody is a valid and valuable exercise in itself and can help contain a client who is all over the place.

So, on that positive note....

REFERENCES

1. Allen, H. (1987) *Gender Unbalanced: Gender, Psychiatry & Judicial Decisions*, OUP
2. Blackburn, R. (1993) 'Crime & Mental Disorder', in *The Psychology of Criminal Conduct*, John Wiley
3. Gunn, J., Maden, A. and Swinton, M. (1991) *Mentally Disordered Prisoners*, Home Office
4. Hodgkins, S. (ed.) (1993) *Mental Disorder and Crime*, Sage
5. Home Office (1990) *Provision for Mentally Disordered Offenders*, Circular 66/90
6. Home office (1991) *Mentally Disordered Remand Prisoners*
7. Home Office (1993) *A Profile of Mentally Disordered Offenders in the Approved Probation and Bail Hostel System*
8. Howels, K. and Hollin, C.R. (eds.) (1993) *Clinical Approaches to The Mentally Disordered Offender*, John Wiley
9. Hudson, B., Cullen, R. and Roberts, C. (1993) *Training for Work with Mentally Disordered Offenders: Report of the Training Needs of Probation Officers and Social Workers*, CCETSW
10. Laing, R.D. and Esterson, R. (1964) *Sanity, Madness and the Family.*
11. Littlewood, R. and Lipsedge, M. (1989) *Aliens & Alienists: Ethnic Minorities & Psychiatry*, London: Allen Unwin
12. NACRO (1990) *The Resettlement of Mentally Disordered Offenders*
13. NACRO (1991) *The Imprisonment of Mentally Disordered Offenders*
14. NACRO (1992) *Revolving Doors*
15. Prins, H. (1980) *Offenders, Deviants or Patients? An Introduction to the Study of Socio-Forensic Problems*, Tavistock
16. Prins, H. (1986) *Dangerous Behaviour, The Law & Mental Disorder*, Tavistock
17. Prins, H. (1990) *Bizarre Behaviours: Boundaries Of Psychiatric Disorder*, Routledge
18. Rack, P. (1991) *Race, Culture & Mental Disorder*, Routledge
19. Reed, J. (Chair) (1992) *Review of Health and Social Services for mentally Disordered Offenders and Others requiring Similar services: A Report of the Staffing and Training Advisory group*, DoH and Home Office
20. Royal College of Psychiatrists (1990) *Psychiatric Practice and Training in British Multi-ethnic Society*, Council Report CR 10
21. Szasz, T. S. (1977) *The Myth of Mental Illness*, Paladin
22. Tonak, D. (1992) 'Mentally Disordered Offenders & The CJA 1991', in *NAPO Journal*, June 1992
23. Tumin, Judge Stephen (1994) Wakefield Prison Report, Chief Inspector of Prisons
24. Worrall, A (1990) 'Treatable Women?', in *Offending Women*, Routledge

8

Domestic violence

The very term domestic violence is a shocking one, juxtaposing as it does two words which normally evoke very different emotions and images. The reality for many women and children is that the home is not a place of sanctuary, security and peace, but is a place of threat, intimidation and violence. The Metropolitan Police receive around 1000 calls a week from women who are experiencing abuse and violence in the home, and the number of reported assaults has increased by 100 per cent between 1985 and 1992. One in five of all murder victims is a woman killed by a current or former partner.

The term domestic violence encompasses a variety of abuse – physical and sexual violence, threats and intimidation, humiliation and put-downs, degradation – behaviour used by some men to get their own way, to punish or to gain control over women.

In all areas of their work probation officers will meet both perpetrators of domestic violence (predominantly men) and those experiencing such abuse (predominantly women). Domestic violence may not be the presenting problem or the current offence, it may be hidden but it is widespread. Perpetrators will often deny the existence or extent of their behaviour in an attempt to present a more favourable image to themselves and others. Those experiencing abuse are often reluctant to acknowledge it from a sense of shame or guilt, or for fear of stigma or the disbelief of others. As with all aspects of probation work, it is essential to be alert to possibilities, to pick up clues and to be aware of what is being said non-verbally. From the various studies which have been conducted into the causes of family violence it is possible to identify factors which are often present in situations of domestic violence. The presence of such factors does not necessarily indicate domestic violence but should alert the worker to the possibility. The more of the factors that are present, the more likely is the possibility.

❑ Predictive characteristics of domestic violence

1   There is a history of violence, threatening behaviour or use of weapons.

2 Exposure to violence as a child.

3 Feeling of low self-esteem and helplessness.

4 Isolation and lack of social support.

5 Feelings of jealousy and accusations of infidelity.

6 Non-accidental injuries such as scratches and black eyes.

7 Presence of a provocative partner who escalates arguments and reciprocates aggressively.

8 Presence of an over-dependent partner, for instance due to poor health, sexual difficulty, or problems during pregnancy and childbirth.

9 There is a history of drug or alcohol abuse.

10 There is a history of psychological disorder such as anxiety and depression.

11 Children with behavioural difficulties, especially anti-social behaviour.

12 Socio-economic difficulties – unemployment, debts.

13 Stress at work or job dissatisfaction.

14 A recent traumatic life-event such as separation or death of somebody close.

❑ The effects of domestic violence on women

Women experiencing domestic violence will frequently be subject to other additional sources of severe stress such as financial difficulties, physical illness, problems with children, accommodation, alcohol and drug misuse (Finn, 1985) and these might well be drawn to the probation officer's attention before domestic violence is detected or admitted. Each woman's experience of domestic violence is, of course, unique but many describe feelings in common of helplessness, of depression, of being unable to do anything to bring about any change, of being to blame and of being worthless. Studies (Finn 1985) have suggested that the greater the stress experienced by a woman, the less likely she is to seek positive ways of coping, such as gaining the support of others, and the more likely she is to act passively – tending to withdraw and learning to endure and adapt to the abusive situation. Women who are repeatedly abused perceive their options gradually to decrease to the point where they believe it is impossible for them to effect any change whatsoever. There are many other understandable reasons why women do not escape their abusers:

- they may lack the resources to do so;

- their first language may not be English;

- they may fear exclusion from their community due to religious/ cultural beliefs;

- they may fear losing their children, a particularly real fear for lesbian women and those with disabilities;

- they may fear even more severe violence or death if they attempt to do so.

Awareness has been growing in recent years about the impact of domestic violence on children, although there remains a dearth of research evidence. Leighton (1989) reported that in 68 per cent of incidents of violence against the mother, a child witnesses the assault, and Hughes (1992) found that in 90 per cent of incidents children are in the same or next room. The effects upon children will obviously vary and depend upon a wide range of factors including age, the quality of relationships, alternative support systems, the frequency and severity of the violence. Many women's aid refuges now employ therapists specifically to work with children.

It is important that probation officers bear in mind that Jaffe et al. (1990) and Hughes (1992) have reported that in at least one in three families where the mother is being abused, at least one child is also the victim of direct abuse.

❏ Working with women

Some probation officers would say that it is rare to meet a woman client who has not experienced abuse either as a child or an adult. With the exception of those women convicted of attacking or killing their partners, however, there is unlikely to be a clear link between their abuse and the offending behaviour which has brought them into contact with the service. Nevertheless, there is almost certain to be an interrelationship. The experience of domestic violence is likely to be so fundamental to the way in which they live their lives and perceive themselves, that it would arguably be impossible to bring about changes in other areas of their life while leaving this untouched.

In working with women who are living with violent partners, it will be necessary to intervene on several levels. In order that she might begin to take some decisions about the way forward a woman will need practical advice and information about the following:

Refuges

These are places of safety available at times of crisis to women and their children and most are affiliated to the National Women's Aid Federation. In order that they might remain places of safety for women, addresses are kept secret and it is important that probation officers have to hand the appropriate telephone numbers. Women are likely to use a refuge in different ways depending on their needs. Some may stay for a short period as a respite from the situation at home, some will use it as a stepping-stone to a new life and will stay until they have alternative accommodation. Refuges are shared houses and women frequently gain considerable support from each other. There are workers available who will advise on such matters as benefits, housing, schooling etc.. In some areas there are refuges specifically for black and Asian women.

The police and the courts

There has long been criticism of police practice in relation to domestic violence, but in recent years there has been some improvement and many forces have followed the Metropolitan Police who in June 1987 issued a force order that domestic violence is to be treated as severely as any other criminal assault. In recent years there has been a greater emphasis on arrest and removal of the perpetrator and on the keeping of statistics and records. In some areas there are specialist domestic violence units, with which it is important that local probation officers make links. They are staffed by women police officers who will retain close contact with women experiencing domestic violence, offering them practical advice and supporting them through the court process in the event of the perpetrator being charged. Whether or not there is a domestic violence unit, however, it is important that women are aware that they can ask the police to:

- interview them separately from the violent man;
- arrange medical treatment;
- give information about refuges;
- accompany them back to the home to collect belongings; and
- keep a record of all incidents of domestic violence against them.

Domestic violence can result in the perpetrator being arrested and charged with a variety of offences: common assault, actual bodily harm, grievous bodily harm, malicious wounding, criminal damage, offences under the Public Order Act, rape, indecent assault and murder. Legislation in 1984 making spouses compellable witnesses and the establishment of the Crown Prosecution Service two years later have increased the incidence of prosecutions for domestic violence. But a large body of research evidence, both from Britain and the United States, suggests that the changes are slow in coming and rates of arrest are only around 15 per cent, with the police still preferring other methods of intervention, such as separating the parties for a period of 'cooling off'. Some studies here, as recently as 1990, show a disappointing tendency on the part of the police actively to discourage women from pursuing a prosecution (Sanders 1988; Bourlet 1990).

In the event of a woman not wishing to pursue matters through the criminal courts, or the police refusing to make an arrest, she has the option of seeking protection from the civil courts by way of an injunction. Women, both married and unmarried, can apply to the county court for a non-molestation injunction ordering the perpetrator not to assault, molest or harass her or her children or an ouster injunction to remove him from the home (Domestic Violence and Matrimonial Proceedings Act 1976). Only a married woman can apply to the magistrates' court for either a Personal Protection Order or an Exclusion Order under the Domestic Proceedings and Magistrate's Courts Act 1978. These orders have the same effect as those issued in the county court. If the court sees evidence of a woman's injuries, it can attach a power of arrest to the injunction which renders it more effective. If the man breaches it, he will be arrested by the police and brought before a court within 24 hours for contempt of court. Imprisonment or a fine will follow.

A woman can apply directly to the courts for an injunction but might prefer to get some legal advice which, if on benefit or low income, she will be able to do without charge under the 'Green Form Scheme' operated by many firms of local solicitors or at a law centre. For a woman whose immigration status might be affected, such as those in Britain on a temporary visa, it is very important to seek legal advice before starting proceedings.

Legal advice is also, of course, vital to those women who fear that their children might be abducted and, at a later stage once the crisis is passed, contact with a local mediation service may be of value in negotiating how the children are to go between their parents in the least traumatic manner.

Accommodation and finance

Many women are trapped in violent situations by lack of access to financial resources and so it is essential that probation officers are able to advise on what they might be entitled to – income support, family credit, child benefit, housing benefit and the social fund if they are to leave home. Applications for benefit can take a while to process, and women who have no money to pay in advance for bed and breakfast or a hostel may apply for a crisis loan.

Under Part III of the Housing Act 1985, local authorities have a duty to make available accommodation for anybody who is homeless, in priority need and has not made themselves intentionally homeless. A woman is deemed to be in priority need if she is pregnant, vulnerable or has dependent children. The Department of Environment Code of Guidance on Homelessness suggests that women without children who are experiencing domestic violence should be considered 'vulnerable' and so in priority need. It goes on to say that women who have had to leave their homes because of violence should never be declared intentionally homeless. Local authorities interpret the law differently and vary in their generosity, so women who already feel exhausted and powerless may need considerable support and assistance in the often frustrating negotiations with the housing department.

In addition to practical advice and information, women are likely to require support and counselling from probation officers if they are to overcome feelings of inadequacy, hopelessness or helplessness. The woman will need to be valued and believed, feeling that she is not being pressured to take decisions, but is being given time and space to explore the possibilities. It will be necessary to assist her in recognising feelings of anger, in identifying her skills and abilities, and in challenging her belief that domestic violence is to be expected in relationships, or that she is somehow to blame for it.

All this is achievable in working with clients on an individual basis, but probation officers have found that women experiencing domestic violence gain considerable support and empowerment from participating in women's groups which provide a forum for sharing experiences and reduce the feelings of isolation and abnormality.

Sonia is currently on probation for several offences of cheque book fraud. She has been living for two years with Frank, who we first encountered in Chapter 2, and is expecting a baby in two months time. There have been numerous incidents of violence over the last two years and Frank has been charged on two or three occasions. Sonia has left Frank several times but he always persuades her to come back. They have recently been reconciled, yet again, with her accepting Frank's protestations that things will be different now because of the baby. They have recently moved to a new area to make a fresh start.

During the course of putting together her supervision plan, Sonia has been determined that her relationship with Frank is no longer an issue. She points to the fact that they have moved away from her family, with whom Frank did not get on well, and they are both looking forward to the new baby. This poses quite a dilemma for the probation officer who is concerned that Sonia sees herself as having some responsibility for the violence – it was her relationship with her family that was the problem, it was she who wanted to go out when all Frank wanted was an evening in etc..

Another concern is that Sonia sees herself as having little worth or identity separate from Frank – he's the one destined for great things and he is always telling her that the only way she will make anything of herself is if she sticks with him…. Does the probation officer accept or challenge Sonia's view that everything will be alright now?

Clearly, the prospect of a baby coming into this potentially volatile situation needs to be addressed. In addition, the worker may have to acknowledge and struggle with her own feelings of frustration and impatience with Sonia – why can't she recognise that he won't change? Why does she keep having him back? Can't she see that she'd be much better off without him?

This situation raises some complex issues. Clearly, simply waiting for the next incident to happen is not the answer, even supposing that Sonia is able to talk about it, which would rather spoil the rosy picture she has painted. If the decision is to work with Sonia on an individual basis, then it will be necessary to establish the sort of relationship within which she feels valued, respected and taken seriously, before she will be able gently to explore the reality of her situation. This will include talking about the history of previous incidents of violence, the evidence she sees of changes in Frank's behaviour, and issues of power and responsibility.

It may be, however, that for Sonia, joining a women's group would be a more helpful way forward. This may help her to form links in a new area where she is isolated. Sharing experiences with other women may assist her to see her relationship with Frank for what it really is, and to place responsibility where it properly lies. It is to be hoped she might also gain the support and confidence necessary to take action should she so wish.

Whatever approach is taken, and whatever progress is made in the work, the issue of the risk posed to the child must be addressed. Strategies for protecting the new baby will need to be discussed with both Frank and Sonia. If the probation officers concerned felt that these were insufficient, then the question of referral to social services for a pre-birth case conference would arise. Otherwise GP, hospital, health visitors will need to be alerted as vigilance on everybody's part will be crucial.

Having considered the way forward with Sonia, it is important to recognise that there will be cases in which the probation officer may feel it appropriate to take a more assertive line in advising the women to leave a potentially dangerous or life threatening situation.

In their evidence to the House Of Commons Home Affairs Select Committee Enquiry into Domestic Violence, The Women's Aid Federation was critical of the probation service for its failure to notify women of significant events such as the home leave or parole of a perpetrator of domestic violence. However, the revised national standards for through care have addressed this, and in cases involving serious sexual or violent offences the supervising service must now contact the victim or victim's family within two months of sentence and offer them the opportunity of being kept informed of the sentence. Where they indicate a wish to be kept informed, the supervising officer must ascertain any concerns prior to preparing a pre-discharge or parole assessment report.

❏ Working with men

As is the case with other violent and sexual offenders, the perpetrator of domestic violence is likely to 'touch' the probation officer personally and to evoke a range of negative feelings – anger, revulsion, contempt. If the probation officer is to work constructively, and not to punish the client unintentionally, then these feelings must be identified and explored, and use of supervision becomes crucial. The line between confrontation and persecution can be a very fine one. Male probation officers may face an additional hazard due to their own socialisation in a fundamentally sexist society – that of collusion with the client, particularly in his playing down of the seriousness of what he has done, or his view of the woman's culpability. It is important that such aspects are anticipated and again explored in supervision.

A growing awareness of the extent of domestic violence and the increasing incidence of convictions in recent years has resulted in some services establishing specialist provision for perpetrators, often in the form of groups where participation may be a condition of probation or parole. Methods are often based upon those pioneered by the Change Project in Stirling, Scotland, the Everyman Centre in Stockwell, London or the Duluth Project in the United States. While it is recognised that a groupwork setting provides certain advantages such as mutual support, (Gondolf (1985) found that men identified group support as the most important factor in helping them to change their violent behaviour), varied role models and sources of feedback, there is no reason why the probation officer, working on a one to one basis with a perpetrator, should not employ the same methods to good effect.

As always, a thorough assessment is the first important step in which the client should be asked explicitly about a range of abusive behaviour both physical and psychological. Specialist projects often make use of questionnaires, administered both to perpetrators and their partners, which elicit information about the frequency (e.g. never, rarely, occasionally, frequently) of behaviour such as slapping, punching, kicking, use of weapons, throwing things, threats to take the children or injure pets, sexual abuse, withholding money, preventing social contacts etc..

Information from the man's partner and from the Crown Prosecution Service documentation or court transcript are essential, as it is very common for men to deny the extent, frequency and seriousness of their violent behaviour, or to construct a defence which places blame upon the woman and justifies the abuse. It is important to bear in mind, however, that a partner herself may be wary of revealing full details of the violence, either through fear of retaliation or a belief that this might jeopardise the chances of the relationship continuing, as in Sonia's case. Overcoming this denial and accepting responsibility for their behaviour is an essential prerequisite to changing it, but it is important that confrontational challenge is carried out in a context within which the man will feel supported and valued rather than despised.

It is generally accepted that the causes of domestic violence are complex, probably involving an interplay of various elements such as the early experiences and personality of the perpetrator, his belief system and the way in which he views the world, the dynamics of the family or relationship, and the position of women in a male dominated society. It therefore makes sense that work with perpetrators of domestic violence, either in a group setting or as individuals, should proceed on an number of levels. The following levels tend to emphasise cognitive and behavioural interventions:

Self-observation

Men are encouraged to analyse their behaviour in detail with particular reference to the chain of events which results in a violent incident. This enables them to identify the 'warning signs' and those critical points at which it might be possible to change direction, for instance, by temporarily removing themselves from the situation or responding in an alternative, non-violent, manner. In Frank's case it seemed that he had invariably been drinking prior to every violent incident. It would be tempting to stop there and attribute all that followed to the effects of alcohol – if only Frank stopped drinking then everything would be alright. In the self observation model, though, the idea is to go back as far as possible – what triggers Frank's trips to the pub? In fact, what we discover is that Frank does not drink on a daily basis by any means, but periodically indulges in very heavy drinking bouts. These bouts are preceded by incidents in which he is belittled, made to feel a fool, or suspects that his masculinity is threatened. Instances include being called a 'short arse' by Sonia's brother and being told off in front of fellow workers for making a mistake. Emerging from the pub very much the worse for wear, the next event in the chain is what he perceives as a further rejection or threat – his supper not being on the table, Sonia making a casual remark about a man on a TV programme that she is watching, or Sonia planning a trip to visit her sister without him.

Cognitive restructuring

Perpetrators often possess a rigid set of beliefs about the way in which their partners should behave which allows them readily to place the blame on their partners should they 'transgress'. Men are encouraged to analyse their thinking patterns and to explore the origin and basis for such beliefs. This will also include an examination of social, cultural and political issues focussing upon gender power and control: How are men socialised? Who are their role models? What is regarded as success? etc.. In addition they will be encouraged to examine the effects of domestic violence on women and children with a view to developing empathy and also to explore gains and losses to themselves.

Some would argue that this work is more effectively undertaken by male officers, as given the strength of gender socialisation it is very threatening for male offenders to explore such sensitive issues in the presence of women. Some groups which run with male only leaders will, however, make a point of having women consultants.

Frank's attitudes and beliefs about what it means to be a man and what it means to be a woman are not unusual and are the product of his socialisation – being brought up in a patriarchal society and exposed to a myriad of models and messages about masculinity, at home, at school, in the media. A questioning and exploratory approach was effective with Frank, rather than one of confrontation which would probably have led to his becoming defensive and more entrenched in his ideas. In addition, it was important at all stages to provide time for Frank to explore and express his feelings about what he was discovering, particularly in connection with his family and early experiences. What is revealed is that Frank's beliefs are consistent with what Brannon and David (1976) identify as the four major expectations of men in society:

The sturdy oak   Frank believes that men should sort things out for themselves, not needing help or being dependent on anybody; they should keep their troubles to themselves and be responsible for their women folk and children who should depend on them. He is able to identify this as very much his father's way, his father being a jealous man of few words, who revealed little of his feelings and believed that what went on within the home was the business of nobody else.

No sissy stuff   Frank believes that men should not cry or talk about their feelings, and that there are many activities which are definitely not appropriate for men and many likewise which are not appropriate for women. Frank's heroes are a professional boxer, and his uncle who is doing nine years for an armed robbery.

The big wheel   Frank believes that men should be the bread winners, successful at work and head of the household; if Sonia sticks with him she will be alright.

Give 'em hell   Frank believes that a man must be able to stand up for himself and not be made to look stupid – you don't let people walk all over you – only wimps take it lying down. When he was bullied at school they said he ran 'like a girl', and he was told at home that he must learn to hit back, or preferably, hit first.

Interpersonal skills training

This is broadly educative with men being taught skills of conflict resolution, assertiveness and relaxation, thus equipping them to defuse stressful situations and behave in an alternative, non-violent, manner.

You will remember that Frank's trips to the pub, which usually preceded a violent incident at home, were often themselves preceded by a situation where he felt put down or perceived that he was made to look foolish. He'd feel inadequate, self-conscious and angry inside, experience physical symptoms – sweating and an increased heart beat – and instead of dealing assertively with the situation, he'd head for the pub to get 'well tanked up' at the earliest opportunity possible. Teaching Frank some simple relaxation techniques, coupled with some skills in assertiveness will provide him with an alternative way of behaving in such situations. So for instance, he might in future recognise the physical signs and take action – breathing deeply, letting the tension out of his muscles, before telling his boss calmly and directly what he feels about being reprimanded in public and asking that it is not repeated in the future.

So Frank provides us with yet another example of the difficult path which PO's have to tread between engaging and working effectively with serious offenders and carrying out their responsibilities towards victims and the wider public.

REFERENCES

1. Bourlet, A. (1990) *Police Intervention in Marital Violence*, Oxford University Press

2. Brannon, D. (ed.) (1976) *The Forty Nine Percent Majority*, Mass., US: Addison Wesley

3. Finn, J. (1985) *The Stresses and Coping Behaviours of Battered Women*, Social Casework No.66

4. Gondolf, E.W. (1985) *Men Who Batter; An Integrated approach to stopping wife abuse*, Holmes Beach FL. Learning Publications Inc.

5. Hughes, (1992) 'The Impact of Spouse Abuse on the Children of Battered Women', in *Violence Update*

6. Jaffe, P., Wolfe, D. and Wilson, S.K. (1990) *Children Of Battered Women*, London: Sage

7. Purdy, F. and Nickel, N. (1981) 'Practice Principles for Working With Groups Of Men who Batter', in *Social Work with Groups*, Vol. 4, 1981.

9. Sanders, A. (1988) 'Personal Violence and Public Order: The Prosecution of Domestic Violence in England and Wales', in *International Journal of the Sociology of Law*, Vol 16, 1988.

9
Working with young people

Young people constitute the lion's share of the work of the probation service. Most of the clients of the service are under 30 and many are in their late teens or early twenties, but youth, or adolescence, is not simply a question of chronology – in fact nobody can tell you exactly when it starts or when it ends. The word 'adolescence' describes a period of transition but how long it lasts depends upon whether a young person has the social and economic wherewithal to proceed to the next stage in the life-cycle.

In his study, undertaken in the USA during the great depression, W. F. Whyte (1943) 'hung out' with a group of 'corner boys' in an Italian neighbourhood. As the book proceeds, we realise that Doc and the Nortons are not teenagers but men, some of them in their mid to late twenties, and that they have been hanging out on the same corner for over ten years. They have been doing this because, having no steady jobs, they have no money to pay rent, buy furniture and do all the other things one would need to do to become a 'family man' in Cornerville. They are, as a result, frozen in a state of perpetual adolescence.

There is increasing evidence, both anecdotal and research-based (Hope 1994), of a similar phenomenon here in Britain in the 1990s with the upper age of members of 'teenage' groups rising in some instances to over 30. Quite simply, these men are getting into offending and staying in it longer. Like Doc and the Nortons, they are unable to make the transition from adolescence to higher status adult roles because they simply do not have the means to do so.

David Brindle writes:

> *Fewer than one in eight offenders serving probation is in full time work or training a survey by NAPO suggests today ... The survey was conducted in May among 1,331 offenders on probation in 19 areas of England and Wales. It found that 12 per cent had a full-time job or training place, with another 4 per cent receiving a mixture of income and benefits ... More than 30 of the 75 probation officers in the survey reported that over 90 per cent of their clients were dependent upon benefits ... People on probation are twice as likely as other jobless to be long-term unemployed. (No-work plight for probationers, The Guardian, 16 Aug 1993)*

Enforced adolescence means that young people on the social and economic margins are, quite literally, prevented from growing up. This has important implications for their involvement in crime because all the evidence we have suggests that 'growing up', the assumption of adult roles, rights and responsibilities, also means growing out of crime (Rutherford 1986). This has clear implications for the work of social workers and probation officers involved with young people in trouble.

We turn, in a moment, to those questions and issues which are specific to working with young people but we should remind ourselves that we have been talking about young people throughout this book. In other chapters we have considered drink and drugs, and while drink and drug-related offences are not the sole prerogative of the young, young people are certainly over-represented in these offence categories. The most likely perpetrator, and the most likely victim, of a violent offence will be a young man. Similarly, child abuse is far more likely to be perpetrated by young parents or step parents who are themselves emotionally deprived.

❑ What is this thing called youth?

If the truth be known, many a probation officer with a generic case-load has been heard to groan at the prospect of a seemingly interminable period of supervising a bored, reticent and at times monosyllabic adolescent. How are we expected to relate to them? What on earth makes them tick? A little self-reflection can go a long way at such times, and it helps to ask a few questions about the differences between the person you are today and the person you were at 17:

- Do I feel differently?
- Do I think differently?
- Are my values different?
- Are my needs different?

An unrepresentative sample of over 200 social work and health care students aged between 25 and 80 replied, almost unanimously, that the major differences between now and then were on the 'outside'. Now they had more money, more autonomy and more responsibility. But, on the 'inside', their thoughts, feelings, values and needs, were still essentially the same.

Some of them said they were braver, less compromised, more idealistic, more optimistic, freer and, of course, younger then and that this sometimes made them envious of the young people with whom they had to deal professionally, or their own adolescent children. Some said that the struggles with authority, which they first experienced in adolescence, remained unresolved and resurfaced now as ambivalence and indecisiveness about the position they should adopt with a young person engaged in a similar struggle.

The Heineken Effect

Like a well known brand of Dutch beer, young people can reach parts of us which nobody else can. If we are not careful, work with young people can turn us inside out and split us down the middle. It can cause us to act like caricatures of ourselves. Whereas, on the one hand, we may be drawn into collusion with a young person who acts out the battle with authority which we never dared enter at the age of 16, on the other, we may be shocked to find ourselves responding to them in exactly the way our parents did to us, and we vowed we never would. In this context, maturity consists of recognising the immature or stultified parts of ourselves which are evoked by our encounter with a young person, accepting them and deciding how they will be kept under control. Maturity also involves standing back, separating the self from the problem and not getting riled by the inevitable testing out. As Pitts (1990) observes:

> It is hard to overstate the importance for the professional worker of not taking hurtful personal remarks personally. They are seldom, in the first instance at least, directed at us because of who we are but rather because of what we are. Wind-ups are seldom malicious, they are designed as a test to see how far we will go, how much we will take, and importantly, whether or not we have a sense of humour. (Pitts 1990, p. 104)

Most research supports the view, articulated by the mature students cited above, that adolescents are not too dissimilar from adults. Relationships between young people and their parents are more likely to be positive and constructive than, for example, relationships between parents. Some Anglo-American sociologists have emphasised generational conflict and the tensions between the values of the peer group and the values of the family as a defining characteristic of adolescence. Marsland writes:

> The crucial social meaning of youth is withdrawal from adult control and influence compared with childhood. Peer groups are the milieu into which young people withdraw. In at least most societies, this withdrawal to the peer group is, within limits, legitimated by the adult world. Time and space is handed to over to work out for themselves in auto-socialisation the developmental problems of self and identity .... (Marsland 1987, p. 12)

In Britain, at least, this radical separation of the generations is not, in fact, the norm. The research evidence indicates that young people in general, and working class young people in particular, usually share their parents' values and spend a great deal of time with them. They seldom reject either the parents' or their values in favour of the 'alternative' values of the peer group. Rutter et al. (1976) found that only four per cent of the parents surveyed in his study felt an increase in alienation between themselves and their children during adolescence. Young people's familial and social class affiliations tend to be far stronger than their affiliation to their generation or to their peer group. However, it may well be that young people in touch with the probation service have more tenuous links with their families and may, in consequence, be more reliant upon their peer group.

Psychoanalytic theory, according to Coleman (1992), identifies the three key characteristics of adolescence thus:

> In the first place adolescence is seen as being a period during which there is a marked vulnerability of personality, resulting primarily from the upsurge of instincts at puberty. Second, emphasis is laid on the likelihood of maladaptive behaviour stemming from the inadequacy of the psychological defences to cope with inner conflicts and tensions. Examples of such behaviour include extreme fluctuations of mood, inconsistency in relationships, depression, and non-conformity. Third, the process of disengagement is given special prominence. This is perceived as a necessity if mature emotional and sexual relationships are to be established outside the home. (Coleman 1992, p. 13)

It is a period of change, psychologically, emotionally, physically, and intellectually. Erikson (1965) described the developmental battle as being between identity and role-confusion, the former being sought and the latter being endured. In the normal course of events a young person will experiment with various selves, ways of being and ways of thinking until some kind of integration occurs combining all the bits that feel compatible and they feel comfortable about the way they are. That is apparently what maturity looks like!

Problems occur when the contradictions between what is going on inside and outside are extreme; when the pressures and demands on the young person are so great, the muddle of options so enormous, and the support systems non-existent or inadequate that there is a complete confusion about identity. Think of Lance in Chapter 5. His parents were very much pre-occupied with their own marital problems, unable to support him in his emotional turmoil and he turned to alcohol. At its most extreme, the confusion of adolescence can result in a breakdown.

However, there is no evidence to suggest that adolescents, in general, suffer from psychopathology more than other age group. Siddique and D'Arcy (1984) summarise the results of their study as follows:

> For the majority, the adolescent transition may be relatively smooth. However, for a minority it does indeed appear to be a period of stress and turmoil. The large majority of adolescents appear to get on well with adults and are able to cope effectively with demands of school and peer groups. They use their resources to make adjustments with environmental stressors with hardly visible signs of psychological distress. (Siddique and D'Arcy 1984, p. 471)

Again, young people involved with the probation service are probably more likely to experience identity crises and mental disorder, and it is obviously important that we do not simply attribute these signs of distress to 'a stage they're going through'.

Perhaps a key defining feature of adolescence is its vulnerability to adult stereotyping. It will doubtless come as a surprise to many to learn that adolescents are significantly less promiscuous than adults and that peer groups are more likely to apply pressures towards sexual continence than sexual experimentation. The unheeded words of Eppel and Eppel (1966) echo down the years:

> The picture that has emerged of this group of young working people [15-17 years of age] is that most of them regard themselves as belonging to a generation handicapped by distorted stereotypes about their behaviour and moral standards. Many feel this so acutely that they believe whatever goodwill they may manifest is at best not likely to be much appreciated and at worst may be misinterpreted to their disadvantage. (Eppel and Eppel 1966: 213)

In addition to the disadvantages which young people in trouble share with some other young people, they often have other, quite distinct, problems. They are, for example, far more likely to be homeless and to be living in poverty. This is a problem which has been exacerbated by recent changes in the benefit entitlements for young people living away from the parental home. They are far more likely to have spent time in local authority care, to have been physically or sexually abused and to have been neglected, rejected or abandoned. They will probably be poorly educated and a proportion of them will be effectively illiterate and innumerate. A disproportionately large number of these young people will be black and their experience of racism may well have compounded the other disadvantages they suffer. They will probably have few close relationships and many of them will abuse, or be dependent upon, drugs, alcohol and other substances.

❏ Young people and the criminal justice system

The Criminal Justice Act 1991 replaced the former Juvenile Courts with Youth Courts and extended their jurisdiction to include 17 year olds who had previously appeared in the adult court. The 16 and 17 year olds are now the joint responsibility of the social services and probation service, and how services for these young offenders are managed and delivered depends upon local negotiations. Some areas have gone as far as developing joint juvenile justice teams staffed by workers from the two agencies, whereas others have opted for separation but close liaison. In any case, many probation areas have recognised the distinct needs of young people and have designated youth teams or youth workers to practise specifically with those under 21.

The Criminal Justice Act also amended the sentencing framework giving courts the power to make probation orders, supervision orders, community service orders, and combination orders in respect of both 16 and 17 year olds. Decisions about who should hold the order – a social worker or probation officer – are negotiated locally and often this will depend upon issues such as previous record of offending and previous involvement with one agency or the other.

In their day-to-day work with young people POs may well be faced with some or all of the following:

- questions of identity and feelings of self worth;
- status frustration;
- isolation and loneliness;
- questions about sexual and gender identity, masculinity and femininity;
- questions about relationships with parents, partners and, sometimes, the young people's own children;
- the emotional consequences of neglect, rejection, abuse and abandonment;
- low educational attainment;
- anger;
- sadness;
- despair;
- violence;
- self-harm;

- bullying;
- racism;
- sexism;
- financial problems;
- housing problems and homelessness; and
- problems of addiction.

Although not necessarily in that order, one at a time, or expressed in words.

As is the case with other young people, the problems young people in trouble face are often a product of the circumstances in which they find themselves and the attitudes of the adults with whom they come into contact; problems which, more often that not, come from the 'outside' rather than the 'inside'. This would, on the face of it, suggest a practice which, in part at least, attempted to make an impact upon these outside circumstances.

A sophisticated national study conducted by the University of Constanz in West Germany, using a mixture of data collected over a thirty year period and its own survey data, has produced important evidence about the effectiveness of working on outside factors. The researchers found that, in the case of serious and persistent young offenders, probation can be remarkably effective in reducing or eradicating offending if, within the first 12 weeks of the probation order the probationer is helped to find adequate accommodation, to organise their finances, to confront or stabilise their addictions, and to form or sustain a relatively secure emotional relationship with another person (Speiss 1994).

While acknowledging that one cannot simply apply German research findings to British practice, this research raises interesting questions about the weighting given to different aspects of the probation task. Could it be, perhaps, that we should use the first 12 weeks of contact with a young person as a period in which a great deal of energy is ploughed into stabilising those aspects of the young person's material, social and emotional world which appear, from the evidence, to be most closely associated with their propensity to re-offend? Would this mean that less emphasis would be placed upon 'confronting offending behaviour', and that this might be something which is approached towards the end of a young person's order?

David Downes (1994) contends that changes to the justice systems make little impact upon crime rates, whereas the quality of the 'ancillary belt of supporting services' which surround the justice system does, and many probation youth teams work very closely with a range of other agencies. It is not unusual for workers from the local health, drug and alcohol, education, training, and employment agencies to run sessions in conjunction with a probation youth team. In addition, a variety of other resources are often made available such as black empowerment groups, specialist interest groups (photography, sport, car maintenance, parenting etc.) or groups focussing on masculinity and offending.

❏ Inter-agency co-operation

Whilst inter-agency work undoubtedly has a lot to offer in the field of youth justice, it is not without its pitfalls. A feature of work with socially marginalised or emotionally deprived young people is the degree of conflict it can sometimes generate between professional workers within a team, an agency or between agencies. This is not the place to explore the extent to which conflictual professional relationships are simply mirroring the nexus of conflictual relationships in which they are required to intervene. What is clear, however, is that such conflict militates against the best interests of the young people involved.

In high stress situations, differences of opinion between workers about the most appropriate form of action can come to assume a far greater significance than they would, on the face of it, appear to merit. What might, in other circumstances, be seen as helpful advice can, in this situation, be received as unwarranted criticism and interference. The ever-present tendency for those with case responsibility to minimise risks can result in them resenting the 'interference' of 'outsiders' who have nothing to lose. Even where responsibility is shared, anxiety can heighten disagreements about the value and likely outcomes of the strategies proposed. One of the consequences of this can be that in a situation which may require unity, some workers will be more committed to a joint strategy than others.

These problems are compounded when there is no mechanism for resolving disputes or negotiating a compromise between professional peers. If discussions reach an acrimonious stalemate, the idea of a shared strategy may soon be abandoned or the problem pushed up the hierarchy for an inevitably unsatisfactory, management decision. If this latter option is pursued, it then becomes possible to blame 'management' for yet another "bloody stupid decision" and this can then reunite the professionals in their opposition to it.

❑ Practice

What all this adds up to is a plea for openness and honesty between agencies and team members and a commitment to shelving the 'macho-correctionalism' which characterises the professional style of some workers with young people in trouble. Some young people will test the boundaries of the professional relationship very vigorously by presenting threatening or even self-damaging behaviour to workers. This often makes workers frightened, yet as professionals they feel that they should be able to cope. As a result, unless they are able to be honest about their apprehensions, they may develop a variety of, not always very useful, strategies to cope with the onslaught of the young person and the fear and anxiety it induces. As we note in Chapter 3, which deals with violence and aggression, denying our anxieties about the people with whom we work does nobody any good, and impairs the capacity of the individual, the team and the agency to work effectively in high risk situations.

Good practice involves having space to work creatively and take calculated risks with young people who might be difficult to engage, in the knowledge that managerial and peer support and professional supervision are available.

Effective teams adhere closely to the principle that confidentiality is to the agency and share information about positive developments in young people's lives as well as questions of dangerousness, violence or abuse. Information should be communicated systematically, rather than inadvertently, to all team members, including administrative staff.

Effective teams negotiate their roles and the boundaries they intend to maintain in their work with individual clients. Many of the young people with whom the probation service has contact have never been given accurate feedback about themselves and the impact of their behaviour. They have not experienced the imposition of realistic and consistent boundaries so a coherent response from all team members is crucial.

We mentioned the Heineken effect earlier. Well, that is made up of several different factors and can appear in a variety of different guises:

1 First, there is the risk of over-identification with the young person who reminds us of ourselves when we were that age. Suddenly we are back there, two adolescents together. This might be quite good fun for the worker but really not what is needed by the client. Think of Lance again – he had plenty of mates in the pub, he didn't need another one. What he was short of was a dependable, consistent adult.

2 Then there's collusion. If we have failed to resolve our own adolescent rebellion, there is a risk of unconsciously colluding with the way in which the young person relates to authority.

3 Next there is envy – there they are young, attractive, free, taking risks – OK they may be in court every other week but life as a probation officer is never that exciting. Envy can trigger the old inner controlling voice of adults in our past and we can become punitive, over controlling, unsympathetic and angry.

4 Finally there is frustration – why don't they listen and accept advice? Why don't they talk? Why do they sabotage everything? Why do they do more of the same when it clearly gets them nowhere? If you are not to be driven wild by such frustration, it is important to remember that they are maybe saying something about not being ready to do things, not being ready for the responsibilities of adulthood. Often, rather than advising or fixing things for them, they simply want us to be there. Authenticity is an important part of being there – not pretending to be somebody else, cool, streetwise, one of their mates, but being yourself. This includes acknowledging the authority in your role, so the young person knows where they stand and where the boundaries lie.

❏ Political correctness versus what works

The primary goal of inter-agency and team work is to develop an intervention which eliminates, or at least reduces, the offending of the young people with whom we work. It is not the case however, that these goals can only, or indeed necessarily, be achieved by the highly prescriptive 'programmes' or 'packages' currently on offer in the probation service (Ross, Ross and Fabiano 1988, Davies and Wright 1989, Raynor, Smith and Vanstone 1994.)

In their recent study of the effectiveness of tightly structured exclusively 'offence focussed' programmes, the Netherlands Ministry of Justice concluded that they appeared to have no significant bearing upon a young person's re-offending and were no more effective than conventional probation (Van der Laan 1993). Similarly, there is little evidence that the 'reasoning and rehabilitation' programme of Ross and Fabiano (1988) is effective. Those who have adopted the programme in the UK have expressed a belief that it will be effective and maintain that preliminary results are 'promising'. A more plausible account of the recent popularity of 'reasoning and rehabilitation' and similar programmes is not that they explain offending very well, nor that they reduce it but rather, that they articulate with the ideological messages emanating from the Home Office and the new administrative imperatives placed on the service by National Standards.

Indeed, there are circumstances in which such 'hard headed' confrontations may have serious unintended consequences. As we have noted, a significant minority of the young people dealt with by the probation service have committed violent or sexual offences and may themselves have been the subjects of violence or abuse.

The process by which an abused person becomes an abuser, or a violent person a violator is explicable in terms of a psychological defence mechanism whereby the victim of aggression 'identifies' with the 'aggressor'. Identification with the aggressor, it is argued, enables the abused individual to repress the feelings of terror and vulnerability engendered by their abuse.

To the criticism that although young women are far more likely to be abused than young men, hardly any young women go on to become abusers, proponents of this position would reply that, as a result of differential gender socialisation, young women are far more likely to internalise the experience, developing feelings of self blame, worthlessness, self hatred and sometimes expressing this through self harm. Whereas young men are far more likely to act the experience out.

Now, whatever one may think of this explanation, it is at least as plausible as those which suggest that violent or sexually abusive behaviour is a learnt behavioural pattern which is triggered by social cues given in a situation of company, or that it is a product of 'cognitive lag', a circumstance in which the abuser can't think straight and is therefore unable to choose the right course of action (Ross and Fabiano 1988).

Speculation about the aetiology of particular behaviours is one thing, but responding to them is another, and this is, as it were, the crunch. If the first account of the aetiology of violent and sexually abusive behaviour is correct, then interventions which attempt to confront that 'offending behaviour' will be saying to the perpetrator:

> *You are a pretty hard and dangerous bloke. What you have done has caused you and a lot of other people a great deal of harm. You have caused suffering and heartbreak to your victim and their family and unless you knuckle down and work on alternative behaviours you will remain a hard and dangerous bloke and our only option will be to take you out of circulation.*

Now this is music to the ears of anybody who is locked into a pattern of identification with their abuser, because here is an important official of the criminal justice system confirming that they are what they so desperately need to be.

153

This raises serious questions about whether offence-focussed work, in which the young person's identity as a perpetrator of violent or sexual offences is reinforced, is at all appropriate. An alternative approach would need to return with the young person to the site of their abuse and violation to enable them to take hold of the repressed feeling bubbling under the surface in the present. The task would be to acknowledge these feelings, to help reconstruct an identity as a whole and valuable person, and so transcend and survive the abuse. This was what the probation officer eventually attempted in her work with Lance, who, you will recall, was physically abused by his father in early adolescence.

In a recent thematic inspection of the probation service's work with young offenders aged 16 and 17 (Young Offenders and the Probation Service, September 1994) the inspectors found that, in half the cases, supervision had had a positive impact. They highlighted examples of impressive practice resulting in real change, but also commented on examples of 'unimaginative routine supervision with little indication that the officer had considered what might work best with a teenager'. As we have stressed throughout this book, there are no quick or easy fixes. Like most people with whom the probation service is involved, young offenders lead very complicated lives blighted by poverty, unemployment, discrimination and abuse. Understanding them as individuals, rather than categories of offender, and assisting them to bring about some change is a complex and difficult job.

REFERENCES

1. Blos, P. (1987) 'The Second Individuation Process of Adolescence', *The Psychoanalytic Study of the Child*, No. 22

2. Brindle, D. (1993) 'No Work Plight For Probationers', *The Guardian*, 16 Aug

3. Downes, D. (1994) 'Serious Diversions: Juvenile Crime and Justice in Europe — the Lessons for Britain', *Social Work in Europe*, Vol. 1 No. 2, Aug 1994

4. Davies, M. and Wright, A. (1989) The Changing Face of Probation: Skills Knowledge and Quality, *Social Work Monographs*, University of East Anglia

5. Erikson, E. (1965) *Childhood and Society*, Penguin

6. Hope, T. (1994) Unpublished Paper presented at 22nd Cropwood Round Table Conference *Preventing Crime and Disorder*, Cambridge, September 1994

7. Pitts, J. (1990) *Working with Young Offenders*, BASW/Macmillan

8. Raynor, Smith, D. and Vanstone, M. (1994) *Effective Probation Practice*, BASW/Macmillan

9. Ross, R. R., Fabiano, E. A. and Ross, R. (1989) *Reasoning and Rehabilitation: A Handbook for Teaching Cognitive Skills*, Ottawa: The Cognitive Centre

10. Speiss, G. (1994) 'Diversion from Custody, How Far Can We Go?', *Social Work in Europe*, Vol. 1 No. 2, Aug 1994

11. Van der Laan, P. (1994) 'An Evaluation of Alternatives to Custody for Young People in Holland', *Social Work in Europe*, Vol. 1 No. 2, Aug 1994

12. Whyte, W. F. (1943) *Street Corner Society*, Chicago University Press

10

Postscript:
A rose by any other name...

We have been writing this book during a period of considerable anxiety and uncertainty in the probation service. Even as we cross the last 't' and dot the last 'i', we ponder on whether all references to probation officers will have to be replaced with 'correctional operative' or 'enforcer' before very long. We reflect on the latest genetic research which suggests that criminals can be identified at birth (come back Lombroso, all is forgiven) and whether this, combined with the Dews Report recommendations concerning the recruitment and training of probation officers, can somehow be usefully combined, so that genetic testing is used to identify both 'fixer' and 'fixee'.... Whatever attempts are made, however, to change the name of the service, its staff or the way its personnel are trained, one thing remains certain: the clients will remain the same and so will the problems. This startlingly obvious fact, drawn to our attention by our trusty PRM, means that whoever ends up doing the job, be they ex-paratroopers, admirals of the fleet, or unmarried, inexperienced young gels, they will still have to use all the intelligence, skill, knowledge, authority and sensitivity they can muster in order to respond purposefully to those who commit crimes, in order to help to reduce offending and effectively protect the public.

This takes time – sometimes a lot of time. When we don't have much time, it is essential to know how best to use this precious resource to its full advantage, so that we can gain a sense of the individual and their situation. After all, these are not cases or statistics, they are people. Yes, they are people who have done dangerous, violent, inexplicable or just plain stupid things, but they are people, nevertheless.

Working with such people is far from easy. It requires startling levels of energy, creativity, maturity and above all, 'stickability' – being able to stay with people in a muddle, in pain, for whom, at times, all hope seems lost. It requires working at different levels at the same time – with what you see, and hear, with what you know, suspect and fear, with the practical and emotional realities of people's lives and within the legal framework within which all POs operate. It is akin to keeping your balance in a high wind, while standing on one leg with the Encyclopaedia Britannica balanced on your head. And that's just on the good days....

However clever, imaginative or tenacious we may be, however flexible and frolicsome our methods, we also offer something beyond value and beyond measure to the people with whom we work. As we have seen in many of the preceding chapters, sometimes the most important thing we can do is to be there and make the time to listen and to take someone seriously. To be able to listen to someone's story without imposing your own values, or feeling the need to tell a story of your own, is a rare quality; to be offered this often comes as something of a shock. Sometimes 'being' takes us considerably further than lots of 'doing'. Doing, after all, needs to be purposeful rather than escapist or engaged in to make us feel useful (nothing like a quick rifle through all those important bits of paper on our desk to make us feel better); 'being' is rather more difficult and often makes us feel worse.

As we have seen throughout this book, there are no easy answers to the problems posed by people in trouble and, consequently, there are no quick fix solutions. This is hardly surprising given the complexity of issues that the PO faces, as this book will have illustrated. Problems ranging from drug and alcohol misuse to child protection, as well as balancing working with people to prevent their offending and reducing the risk to the public. Such work demands a very high degree of skill in addition to commitment. The reflective practitioner, at whom this book is aimed, knows that techniques alone do not work, however fashionable they may be and that there is no one approach that works for everybody. The threat of the de-professionalisation of the probation service is of great concern, as, if this occurs, it will begin to undermine the quality of service and dedication that the great majority of PO's bring to their work. Such de-professionalisation, as we saw at the start of this book, has its roots in the politics of criminal justice policy during the 1980s and early 1990s.

Such a climate places pressures on services and workers to react with over-simplistic responses and can result in policies, techniques and models of intervention at the coal face which may be more a reflection of what the agency thinks it needs to sell in order to survive, than that which is actually demonstrably consistent and effective. The art of good practice, after all, lies in the worker's ability to choose from a varied menu of approaches, and to apply them selectively so that they can match the needs, issues and offending presented by each individual. In the same way that a doctor would not just use a stethoscope to establish what a patient needed, a probation officer who can only apply one model is unlikely to have the necessary understanding or resources to work with the variety of problems that are presented.

We suspect at times that the combined impact of cost-effective justice and the need for a defence against the pain and difficulty of the probation officer's task becomes institutionalised and finds expression in some tactics currently in vogue, which tend to address only one aspect of the individual, rather than the complexities that make up the real person. What we have to ask ourselves though, is whether the method has been designed for the convenience of the agency and worker, or reflects a true professionalism that needs defending from arbitrary ideological shifts. What 'works' needs to be defined with honesty and integrity, in addition to the thoroughness of research, otherwise the probation service will continue to respond with expedient measures each time there is another volte face in criminal justice policy.

Appendix 1
Drug law

❏ A basic introduction to the Misuse of Drugs Act

The main piece of legislation dealing with drugs is the **Misuse of Drugs Act 1971**. This divides drugs into categories (**A, B & C**), depending on how dangerous they are thought to be. New drugs can be added to the existing list, thus for example, in 1977 an amendment was introduced to cover all Amphetamine like compounds.

The Act not only lists drugs into categories, but it also defines types of activity in relation to these drugs, which vary in seriousness. Consequently, with regard to certain drugs it is illegal to:

- Just have the drug (**possession**).
- Have the drug to sell/give to others (**possession with intent to supply**).
- Make or grow the drug (**supply**).
- Give, sell or share the drug (**supply**).
- Import or export.
- Allow your home, or premises, to be used for supplying or offering to supply the drug.

Such definitions are often complicated and open to dispute.

The Class category of the drug (i.e. **A, B or C**) is combined with the defined activity engaged in, in order to establish sentences. The amount of the drug involved will, often of course, be the main thing that determines the level of seriousness.

The following table lists some of the main drugs that bring offenders before the courts. It is by no means a complete list. (For a more comprehensive list see, for example; *Drug Abuse Briefing* 1994.) It is important to note that the class category is defined with regard to "how dangerously the **individual** drug is viewed." Thus the generic drug group will, in some cases, include individual drugs which are classified in different class categories.

161

Painkillers

Drug group/type	Principal drug	Class
Opiates (deriving 'naturally' from poppy)	Diacetylmorphine	A
Opioids (synthetic opiates)	Diamorphine or Heroin	A
Narcotic analgesics	Dipipanone (Diconal)	A
	Methadone (Physeptone)	A
	Morphine	A
	Pethidine	A
	Dextromoramide (Palfium)	A
	Buprenorphine	A
	Dihydrocodeine (D.F. 118)	B
	Dextropoxyphene (Distalgesic)	C

Drugs in this group differ very greatly in their strength and effects

N.B. Any class B drug prepared for injection counts as a class A drug.

Stimulants

Drug group/type	Principal drug	Class
Cocaine	Cocaine hydrochloride	A
	Cocaine freebase (Crack)	A
Amphetamine or Amphetamine type drugs	Amphetamine sulphate	B
	Dexamphetamine (Dexedrine)	B
	Methylphenidate (Ritalin)	B
	Diethylpropion (Aspiate, Tenuate)	C
	Phentermine	B

Hallucinogens

Drug group/type	Principal drug	Class
Hallucinogens	Lysergic acid (LSD) Diethylamide or Lysergide	A
Hallucinogenic mushrooms	Psilocybe semilanceata	A *
	Amanita muscaria	A *
Hallucinogenic amphetamines	Methylenedioxy-amphetamine MDMA, MDA, PMA, DOM, (includes Ecstasy, E, etc.)	A
Cannabis	Herbal cannabis (Grass)	B
	Cannabis resin (Hash)	B
	Cannabis oil	B

* N.B. In mushroom form these are not illegal; but if prepared for use, they are classified as class A drugs.

Depressants

Drug group/type	Principal drug	Class
Barbiturates	Quinalbarbitone (Seconal)	B
	Amylobarbitone (Amytal)	B
	Combination of above (Tuinal)	B
	Pentobarbitone (Nembutal)	B
	Butobarbitone (Soneryl)	B
Benzodiazepines (minor tranquillisers)	Nitrazepam (Mogadon)	C
	Flurazepam (Dalmane)	C
	Triazolam (Halcion)	C
	Temazepam (Normison)	C
	Diazepam (Valium)	C
	Oxazepam (Serenid)	C
	Lorazepam (Ativan)	C
	Chlordiazepoxide (Librium)	C

As adapted from ISDD drug abuse chart and *Drug Abuse Briefing* (1994)

❑ Sentencing factors and maximum penalties

The following lists some of the factors affecting sentencing with regard to class A, B and C drugs. We stress that whilst it is useful to keep some of these in mind, they only offer parameters in which to assess the seriousness of the offence. Sentencing policy is not a scientific process. Actual sentencing is affected by other detailed consideration of the particular circumstances of the offence(s) in question, the offender, and their response to previous disposals, where relevant. For cases dealt with at magistrates' court we refer to an entry point as quoted in the Magistrates Association Sentencing Guidelines. The term is used as a guide to magistrates as a starting point for an offence of 'average seriousness', on a first time offender pleading "not guilty" before aggravating and mitigating circumstances have been taken into account.

Class A drugs

Possession

Aggravating factors	Mitigating factors
Any amount other than very small	Very small quantity for personal use

Magistrates' court entry point = community penalty.
Magistrates' court maximum penalty = 6 months imprisonment and/or £5,000 fine.
Crown court maximum penalty = 7 years imprisoment or unlimited fine.

Possession with intent to supply; supplying; production etc.

Aggravating factors	Mitigating factors
Large amount; profits; value	Low amount/value
Evidence of professional operation	Single opportunistic offence
Close to source of supply	Supplying to friends
Supplying vulnerable groups	

No magistrates' court entry point, as usually committed to crown court.
Magistrates' court maximum penalty = 6 months imprisonment and/or £5,000 fine. (But cases would only rarely be dealt with here).
Crown court maximum penalty = Life imprisonment and/or unlimited fine.

Class B Drugs
Possession

Aggravating factors	Mitigating factors
Large amounts	Small amount for personal use

Magistrates' court entry point = Fine
Magistrates' court maximum penalty = 3 months imprisonment and/or £1,000 fine.
Crown court maximum penalty = 5 years imprisonment and/or unlimited fine.

Possession with intent to supply; supplying; production etc.

Aggravating factors	Mitigating factors
Large amount; large profits	Produce or cultivate for own use
Commercial production	No profit from supply
Supplying vulnerable groups	Supplying to friends
	Single opportunist offence

Magistrates' court entry point = Commit for trial unless small scale supply, otherwise custody.
Magistrates' court maximum penalty = 6 months imprisonment and/or £5,000 fine.
Crown court maximum penalty = 14 years imprisonment and/or unlimited fine.

Class C drugs

The law relating to class C is one in which probation officers are less likely to encounter, due to the, generally speaking, less serious breaches of law involved. Thus, more detailed information about sentencing factors is less relevant or readily available. There is some debate about the law and prosecution with regard to possession of class C drugs. For example, it is still not illegal to possess, in medicinal form, Benzodiazepines without a prescription. However, the possession of illicitly produced Benzodiazapines would be an offence.

Supplying or possession with intent to supply, or other activity in relation to manufacture of such drugs is, of course, illegal (see ISDD 1994 *op.cit.* or Release 1991 for more details).

Magistrates' court maximum penalty = 3 months imprisonment and/or unlimited fine.
Crown court maximum penalty = 2 years imprisonment and/or unlimited fine.

REFERENCES

1. Gilyeat, D. (1994) *A Companion Guide to Offence Seriousness*, Owen Wells Publishing
2. Institute for the Study of Drug Dependence (1994) *Drug Abuse Briefing*, 5th Edition ISDD
3. Magistrates Association (1993) *Magistrates Association Sentencing Guidelines*, The Magistrates Association
4. Release (1991) *Drugs and the Law*, Release Publications